IMAGES OF ENGLAND

PLYMOUTH

IMAGES OF ENGLAND

PLYMOUTH

DEREK TAIT

TEMPUS

Frontispiece: The Hoe, 1920s. One of Plymouth's most popular landmarks and tourist attractions, the Hoe has seen generations of visitors. The Naval Memorial can be seen on the left, with Drake's statue in the foreground and the Armada memorial in the background.

First published 2003

Tempus Publishing Limited
The Mill, Brimscombe Port,
Stroud, Gloucestershire, GL5 2QG
www.tempus-publishing.com

© Derek Tait, 2003

The right of Derek Tait to be identified as the Author
of this work has been asserted in accordance with the
Copyrights, Designs and Patents Act 1988.

British Library Cataloguing in Publication Data.
A catalogue record for this book is available from the British Library.

ISBN 0 7524 3128 5

Typesetting and origination by Tempus Publishing Limited.
Printed in Great Britain by Midway Colour Print, Wiltshire.

Contents

The pier and Staddon Heights from Plymouth Hoe, *c.* 1920. The pier was opened on 29 May 1884 and featured slot machines, a stationers and bookstall, a reading room and also a post office. Pleasure steamer trips left from the iron stairways that led down to the water.

Introduction

Plymouth in the late nineteenth century was very different from today's city. There were no cars, no televisions, no radios and no electric lighting. There were no superstores and most groceries were bought from the local corner shop, which would quite often sell rabbit and pheasant along with its usual wares.

Luckily, though, there was photography. Basic photography had its origins in the early nineteenth century. With vast progress by Fox Talbot, the demand for photographs grew. In the 1850s, there were only a handful of photographic establishments, but by the end of the century, there was a craze for photography. Shopkeepers, businessmen and ordinary people would have their images reproduced on postcards to keep or to send to their families. Photographic studios were kept constantly busy and there were many of these in Plymouth. Two-thirds of the photographers in Plymouth in the early twentieth century were situated in Union Street. Few people had their own cameras, so people would visit the photographer to have portraits or family shots taken. Some studios could even accommodate up to fifty people in one photograph. Unfortunately, a lot of these old photographs have been destroyed, either burnt or consigned to the rubbish dump. However, many of these early photographs and postcards have survived and some are reproduced in this book.

Plymouth at the beginning of the twentieth century was effectively three towns: Plymouth, Stonehouse and Devonport. In 1901, the population of these three towns was nearly 193,000. The three towns expanded to take in many rural areas. In 1896, western Peverell and Compton became part of Plymouth and, in 1898, St Budeaux, Saltash Passage and Pennycross became part of Devonport. In 1914, after much disagreement, Plymouth, Stonehouse and Devonport were amalgamated into one town. Plymouth became a city in 1928.

Transport played a big part in linking the towns. Plymouth's first tramway was opened in 1872 by the Plymouth, Stonehouse & Devonport Tramways Company. Before the advent of electricity, the trams were pulled by horses. The 4ft 8in track ran from Derry's Clock, along Union Street, over Stonehouse Bridge and ended at Cumberland Gardens in Devonport. In 1874, the line was extended to run to Fore Street in Devonport. Electric trams took over from the horse-drawn ones in the early 1900s and the service eventually covered most of the area known today as Plymouth.

Plymouth before the First World War was a bustling, vibrant town with many popular shops such as Dingles, Goodbody's, Popham's and John Yeo's. Popham's toy room boasted a stock of 2,000 dolls in 1882 and Goodbody's was famous for its restaurant where the Royal Marines Band would play in the afternoon. Dingles also had its own band, the George East Orchestra.

The people of Plymouth were not short of entertainment. There was a wealth of theatres in the town. There was the Grand Theatre in Union Street, famous for its Christmas pantomimes, the Theatre Royal which opened in 1813, the Palace Theatre of Varieties, which opened in 1898, and the Hippodrome which opened in 1908. The Hippodrome was later converted into a cinema to welcome the arrival of talking movies in 1929. Some of the acts that came to Plymouth included Harry Houdini, Lillie Langtry, Buffalo Bill and Laurel and Hardy.

People could catch a tram or walk to the pier and stroll the boards or watch the many attractions that took place there. The Hoe was alive with entertainment from local military bands, dancing, annual regattas and regular swimming events.

The Second World War turned Plymouth upside down. Plymouth and Coventry were the worst-hit areas in Britain after London and the heavy bombing all but obliterated Plymouth. Food was rationed and, during the blackout, people were afraid to even strike a match for fear of enemy attacks. Thick blackout material could be bought at two shillings a yard and this was used to stop the slightest glint of light escaping from buildings. At night, it was difficult to find your way about or to be seen and it was suggested that more people died from traffic accidents in Britain than from enemy bombing. There were certainly many fatalities due to vehicles travelling with hooded or no lighting. With no street lighting, it was very hard to walk or drive through the town at night.

During bombing, sirens would sound and mothers would take their children to the Anderson shelters in their gardens. Some even headed out into the country and the moors to avoid the bombing. The next day, those who could, got on with their lives, while the homeless were cared for in government rest centres where the Voluntary Service would provide cups of tea and blankets.

Heavy bombing during the Blitz of 1941 changed the face of Plymouth forever. The city was devastated. 1,174 civilians lost their lives and 3,269 were seriously injured. Over 5,000 buildings were destroyed and 80,000 damaged; Plymouth would never be the same again. Major shopping areas like Bedford Street, Spooner's Corner and Old Town Street were reduced to a pile of rubble and many other well-known streets were also completely destroyed. The heart of the city was totally devastated, leaving just St Andrew's Church, the Guildhall (though both very severely damaged), the *Western Morning News* building and the Regent Cinema (now Littlewood's) standing in the main part of the city.

Winston Churchill visited the city in 1941 and when he saw the devasted areas he was said to be visibly shaken. Huge crowds turned out to see him as he toured the remains of the city. Cries of 'Give it to them back!' were heard. There are few surviving buildings or streets of the old city though the Hoe, apart from the pier and bandstand, remains pretty much intact.

Plymouth was seen as a blank canvas on which to start again and work got underway to rebuild the city in 1947. Its main feature, Royal Parade, remains much the same today. By 1959, over £8 million had been spent on land acquisition by the Reconstruction Committee of the City Council. Huge areas of Plymouth had been demolished and rebuilt as new homes and businesses. In the early 1950s, Woolworth's, Dingles, John Yeo's and Timothy White's reopened for business. Plymouth was seen then as a very modern city with its three main shopping streets and the long stretch of Armada Way leading down from the Hoe straight through the centre of the city. Reconstruction finally ended in 1962 with the opening of the Civic Centre by the Queen on 26 July, some twenty-one years after the Blitz.

An ever-growing city, Plymouth is constantly changing and expanding. However, the main city and shops in New George Street, Cornwall Street and Royal Parade have changed little since the reconstruction after the war.

I hope this book will bring back many memories for the older generation and introduce younger generations to the varied and interesting history of Plymouth.

Derek Tait
August, 2003

one

In the Town

George Street, *c.* 1910. Derry's Clock is in the middle of the picture. All trams terminated here and the clock was a common meeting place for young sweethearts, though it was known as the 'four-faced deceiver' because the clocks on all four sides appeared to show different times! Lloyds Bank is on the right. One of the few buildings still standing after the Second World War, it has in recent years become the Bank public house.

Bedford Street, *c.* 1905. Pre-war Bedford Street was a bustling, vibrant street known for its popular shops such as John Yeo's, Dingles and Popham's. John Yeo's were well known for their range of blankets and haberdashery and Popham's for their goods, including jewellery and gloves, aimed at the middle classes. George East and his Trio played in Popham's lavish restaurant and having tea there was compared to having tea at the Savoy.

Opposite below: Lockyer Street, *c.* 1906. The Royal Hotel can be seen on the left. This adjoined the Theatre Royal in George Street. Work was started on the building in 1811 from plans drawn up by John Foulston. It took two years to complete at a cost of £60,000. A casualty of the Blitz, the site was occupied for many years after by a small car park. Opposite the Royal Hotel is the Lockyer Hotel.

Above left: An advertisement for Goodbody's Cafés, *c.* 1932. Goodbody's was a popular café and meeting place at 19-20 Bedford Street, where the Stanton Wicks Orchestra would play daily. They also had smaller cafés at George Street and Mutley Plain before the Second World War. There is still a Goodbody's Café on Mutley Plain.

Above right: An advertisement for Spooner's, *c.* 1932. Spooner's was one of the best-known shops in pre-war Plymouth. Spooner's Corner was a popular meeting place. Like many other shops in the town, they had their own orchestra playing in their restaurant. The shop featured its own fashion department, which took up one floor, and it even had its own theatre to perform fashion parades. In 1902, Spooner's was seriously damaged by a fire when a shop assistant accidentally set fire to a display commemorating the coronation of King Edward VII. Spooner's survived until the Blitz of 1941 and was eventually rebuilt on Royal Parade.

Opposite below: The Guildhall interior, *c.* 1910. The great hall, which measured 146ft by 58ft, was totally destroyed by the bombing of 1941 and it took another ten years to decide whether to rebuild or demolish it completely. It was finally decided to rebuild it and it was reopened in 1959, some eighteen years later.

The Guildhall, right, taken from an etching, *c.* 1887. The Guildhall was built between 1870 and 1874 at a cost of £50,000. It was almost completely destroyed by the Blitz of 1941 when only its outer shell remained. It was originally built by a local man, John Pethick, who later became Mayor in 1898.

Guild Hall, Plymouth.

75521. (W.)

George Street and the Theatre Royal, *c.* 1915. The landmark of Derry's Clock can be seen clearly in this picture. It survived the Blitz and still stands behind the new Theatre Royal. There have been many suggestions about moving it but it still remains in its original location, though anyone from the turn of the twentieth century viewing it now would have difficulty recognising any of its surroundings.

The General Post Office, centre, *c.* 1910. The post office stood in Westwell Street, looking down from Princess Square, and was a popular port of call. It was opened in 1884 and built of Portland stone at a cost of £16,500. It was designed by E.G. Rivers of Bristol. Its interior was reconstructed in 1933 and it featured an inlaid floor depicting Sir Francis Drake's ship, the *Golden Hind*, and the *Mayflower*. Also featured in this picture are the Guildhall, left, and the Municipal Buildings, right.

An advertisement for Pophams, *c.* 1920. Pophams was a very popular shop in pre–war
Plymouth and was known as the 'Harrods of the West'. It catered for the city's well-
heeled and county set and there was a certain snobbery about being employed there.
After the war and the reconstruction of Plymouth, Pophams reopened on Royal Parade.

An advertisement for Jaeger Wear, *c.* 1920. Situated in Old Town Street, Jaeger Wear
was founded in 1884 by Dr Gustav Jaeger, a zoologist who thought that if animals were
healthy with wool against their skin then humans would be too! The idea was taken up
by an English grocer, Lewis Tomalin, who bought the patent and produced 'Dr Jaeger's
Sanitary Woollen Wear'.

Employees of E. Dingle & Co., 1939. Dingle's were situated in Bedford Street and this photograph shows some of the staff who worked there. They gave up their two weeks' holiday to work on the land as part of the war effort in 1939. Barbara Hill, aged eighteen, is in the middle of the front row, wearing wellington boots.

Opposite below: The Dingle's staff with the landowner on his farm, 1939. During the Second World War, with a shortage of men, who were away fighting, land girls played a vital role in keeping the country going. They took on a wide variety of agricultural work on farms including ploughing, harvesting, haymaking and dairy work.

Right: Western Morning News delivery drivers, 1940. The *Western Morning News* van was a popular sight in Plymouth, delivering newspapers to various shops around the city. Their deliveries continued, in darkness, during the blackouts of the Second World War. On the far left of the photograph is Percy Colton and his brother, Sid, is standing next to him.

Below: An advertisement for R. Cundy & Sons, 1920s. R. Cundy & Sons were better known as the Trafalgar Dairy. They were based at Trafalgar Place in Stoke and had been established since 1820. Their produce included raw milk, cream, butter and eggs direct from their farms.

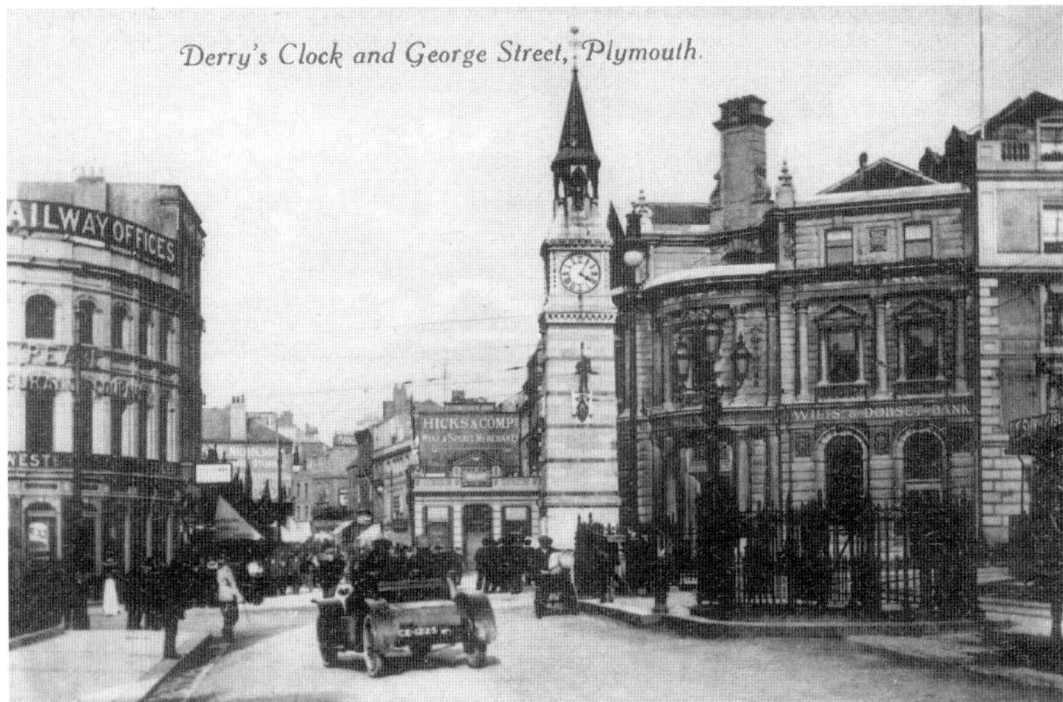

Derry's Clock and George Street, Plymouth.

The parish church of St Andrew and Guildhall Square, 1930s. Before the war, St Andrew's Church was located on the southern side of Bedford Street. A church is believed to have stood on this spot since before 1264. The tower dates from 1461 and the labour to build it was paid for by a wealthy local merchant, Thomas Yogge.

Opposite above: An advertisement for Hicks & Co., *c.* 1920. Hicks & Co. were wine merchants located at 3 Wembury Street. They were suppliers to the Royal Navy, the Army, the Duke of Cornwall Hotel and were also agents for Carr's Cider.

Opposite below: Derry's Clock and George Street, *c.* 1923. Derry's Clock was presented to the town in 1862 by William Derry and was worth £220, which was half the cost it took to build the tower to house it. Plymouth didn't have the powers to build a clock – it had to be approved by Parliament – so Derry's Clock was officially a fountain though it has never been connected to a water supply.

An advertisement for Boots the Chemists, *c.* 1932. The original Boots shop was founded by John Boot in 1849. Boots have had a pharmacy in the city since long before the Second World War. In total, thirty-three Boots chemist shops were destroyed in Britain due to enemy action. Some Boots stores were used as first-aid posts and the staff took civil defence tests and worked as air-raid wardens.

An advertisement for the Three Towns Dairy, *c.* 1932. Even before the war, the Three Towns Dairy would send clotted cream all around the country by post. Many people's first taste of clotted cream would have come from this well-known dairy situated in Union Street. They also had cafés at 52 Union Street and 8 Westwell Street and their advertisement proclaimed 'Devonshire Dainties our Speciality'.

Opposite below: Guildhall and post office, *c.* 1917. Plymouth Chamber of Commerce was first established at the Guildhall on 28 December 1813. Under the trustee of the Earl of Mount Edgcumbe, Lord Eliot, Lord Boringdon, the Duke of Bedford and Mr Carew, MP, their main objectives were to rejuvenate home and foreign fisheries, to begin whale fisheries in the South Seas and Greenland, and to establish a trade with the West Indies for rum, sugar, coffee and molasses. They also planned to regenerate many of the town's old industries.

Old Town Street, *c.* 1905. This area was bombed extensively in the Second World War and the only part of the city that retains the name of Old Town Street is by the main post office at the top of Royal Parade stretching towards New George Street. Before the war, Old Town Street featured many well-known stores, including Woolworth's, Mumford's, La Brasseur and Notcutt the photographers.

Old Town Street, *c*. 1905. Plymouth Chambers can be seen on the left of the picture. Above are the London and Manchester Industrial Assurance offices. Walking down the road is a man with a sandwich advertising board, though you need good eyes to spot him. Old Town Street stretched from Spooner's Corner up to Tavistock Road. In the 1700s, Plymouth consisted of just 1,600 houses, all based around Sutton Harbour. The northern end of the town was where the top of Royal Parade is now and Old Town Street led out into open countryside.

Old Town Street, *c*. 1910. A busy shot of Old Town Street, showing cars and trams running alongside each other. A horse and cart can also be seen in the background. Old Town Street was continually widened over the years for ever-increasing volumes of traffic. The building at the end of the street stood for many years after the war and carried a large sign saying 'Guinness is good for you'.

St Andrew's Church, known as the mother church of Plymouth, *c.* 1910. William de la Stane was the first recorded vicar here in 1264. It is the largest parish church in Devon and is 184ft long and 69ft wide. The morning after St Andrew's was bombed during the Second World War, someone placed a wooden sign over the north door with the word *Resurgam,* meaning 'I will rise again'. The word is now carved in stone above the main door.

St Andrew's Church interior, *c.* 1920. In March 1941, the church became a ruin after a bombing raid on the city. The roof was destroyed and all the fittings were burnt. For a while, the empty shell became a garden church which many people enjoyed visiting. It wasn't until 1949 that repair work was considered, and rebuilding was completed in 1957.

Charles Church, *c.* 1920. King Charles I gave his permission for a new church to be built in Plymouth in 1641 and it was completed in 1658. It was known then as 'the Church of Plymouth called Charles Church'. Its tower was not completed until 1708 and the spire was made of wood covered with lead until 1766. It was bombed in 1941 and its remains can still be found on the Charles Cross roundabout as a memorial to Plymouth's war dead.

St Augustine's Church, Alexander Road, Lipson Vale, *c.* 1920. Work was started on the church in 1899. It was a mission church until it was consecrated in 1905. The church, made of granite and Gothic in style, was completed in 1933. It survived the war and the twentieth century but was demolished at the beginning of the twenty-first.

Union Street, c. 1905. John Foulston designed Union Street in 1911 to link Plymouth with its neighbours, Devonport and Stonehouse. Shops that can be seen in this picture are Oliver's, Wright's hairdressers, A. Levy & Co., The Studio, Posada and on one of the awnings can be seen Halford Cycle Co. At Christmas, Halford's would have a large Hornby railway set laid out in their window which would delight adults as well as children.

Union Street, c. 1905. Famous for its public houses, Union Street became well known all over the world, mainly among the sailors who regularly frequented it. A bustling street, it contained theatres, cinemas, pawn shops, hotels and photographers as well as many general stores. The largest of the twenty or so pubs in Union Street was the Long Room which was remembered for the barmaids who all wore long black dresses.

Union Street Infants' School, *c.* 1905. In the front row, in similar dresses, can be seen four sisters of the Legg family. The Union Street school was situated at Summerland Place and opened on 27 July 1883. By 1888, there were 260 boys, 206 girls and 304 infants attending the school. The headmistress of the infants' school was a Miss Mary Yeo. The school was destroyed by bombing during the Second World War.

Children of Union Street Infants' School, *c.* 1900. You can really get a feel for the Victorian age and its fashions from this photograph. They all look shocked to be having their photo taken! The Education Act of 1870 compelled all children, for the first time, to get a proper education. Powers were given by the government to enforce attendance of children under thirteen and school boards were elected to levy money for fees or to decide whether to teach the children for free.

Union Street, *c.* 1910. Before traffic lights were introduced, policemen on points duty were needed to deal with the ever-increasing flow of traffic. Here, however, is a quieter time when the only traffic appears to be the odd tram and the occasional horse and cart. This is the junction of Union Street by Dunn's. In the background is Oliver's, a boot and shoe shop, Wright's hairdressers and also the Posada, a popular public house that was destroyed during the war.

Union Street, *c.* 1910. A no. 5 tram travels along Union Street, passing the Swiss Café Restaurant which boasted a stock of over 150 wines, both British and foreign. In the distance can be seen an advertisement for Singer's sewing machines. Routly's is on the right.

Tavistock Road, *c*. 1905. This is still recognisable today: not much has changed apart from people's fashions and the disappearance of the trams. Queen Anne Terrace on the right was once the home of many professionals such as doctors. It is now occupied by estate agents and solicitors.

Tavistock Road, *c*. 1905. The Sherwell Congregational Chapel, on the left of the picture, still stands. It was built in 1864. On 13 January 1941, Sherwell Congregational Chapel was the first of Plymouth's churches to be seriously damaged by enemy bombing during the Second World War. The no. 26 tram is on its way to the theatre via Compton.

C.J. Park pharmaceutical chemist, *c.* 1905. Park's chemist was situated on Mutley Plain. Today, the contents of C.J. Park's pharmacy are displayed in the apothecary's room at the Merchant's House, on St Andrew's Street. There were several chemists in the town and many combined photography with dispensing drugs. (Photograph courtesy of the Park Pharmacy Trust.)

An advertisement for Balkwill & Co. Chemists, *c.* 1920. Situated at 106 Old Town Street, they were one of the West Country's oldest chemists and stayed open twenty-four hours a day, every day. They were specialists in fitting trusses, belts and stockings. Try getting that service from your chemist today!

Heath & Stoneman, *c.* 1920. There were many opticians in Plymouth before the Second World War. Heath & Stoneman were located at 24 George Street. They were established in 1848 and a sign outside the shop read: 'Oculist's Prescriptions Dispensed and Repairs Executed in our own Workshop'. They also developed and printed photographs.

Mutley, c. 1910. Mutley comes from two words, 'Gemot' and 'leah', meaning 'meeting place'. This later became 'Motte Leigh' and then finally 'Mutley'. Mutley Plain became Plymouth's secondary shopping centre after the bombing of the city in 1941. This earlier shot shows a quieter time before the two world wars.

Beechwood Avenue, c. 1910. Still very recognisable today, Beechwood Avenue off Mutley Plain has changed very little over the years. Close by is the Royal Eye Infirmary. The building was opened on 30 October 1901 by Lady Mary Parker and cost £18,600 to build. The building was designed by Charles King.

St James the Less Church, *c.* 1912. The church stood behind the Duke of Cornwall Hotel at Clarendon Place in Citadel Road. It was consecrated in 1861 and was completed in 1879. It seated a total of 600 people. Bombed in the Blitz, it was rebuilt at Ham and the old site became St Andrew's Primary School.

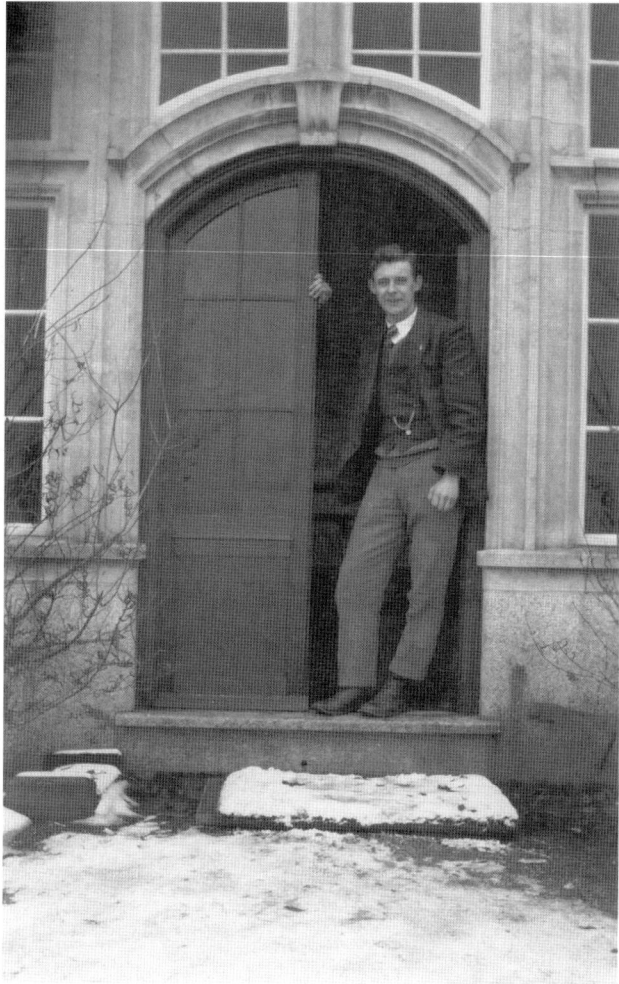

Edward Dart outside St James the Less, 1920. A school stood beside the church and was also destroyed in the Blitz of 1941. In 1868, there were sixty-two boys, fifty-two girls and forty-eight infants at the school. Teaching included the usual reading, writing and arithmetic. Geography and History were added and the girls took needlework and knitting. The boys were also taught drawing and vocal music and the ones with good singing voices were admitted to the church choir.

Opposite below: Spooner's Corner, *c.* 1941. This well-known area of the city lies devastated after the Blitz of 1941. Once a popular meeting place, it had been one of the busiest road junctions in the city. A sign warns of the dangers of the crumbling buildings, though it could be guaranteed that children would explore this and other bombed sites for souvenirs.

She's

FARLEY *fed—*

"She's 'Farley' fed" is a phrase one so often hears from happy mothers with contented and happy children.

Babies and young children thrive on Farley's— and what is so very important of course, is that they really enjoy their feed of Farley's from the first moment they start on "solids".

If ever you wonder why all children love FARLEY'S you should try one yourself, they're delicious.

FARLEY'S RUSKS
— Baby's first solid food —

FARLEY'S INFANT FOOD LTD. · PLYMOUTH · DEVON

Farley's advertisement, *c.* 1947. Farley's rusks have been fed to generations of children over the years and the company name dates back to 1880. This advertisement dates from just after the Second World War. Farley's were a very well-known business in Plymouth and they were eventually taken over by Heinz in 1994.

New George Street, *c.* 1949. After the war, the plan to rebuild Plymouth got under way in March 1947. Before the war, New George Street was part of Frankfort Street. The *Western Morning News* building, Leicester Harmsworth House, can been seen on the left of the picture but the area beside it, that would have been the Costers building, was destroyed by bombing and cleared away. Opposite stood the Regent Cinema (later Littlewood's).

Above: John Yeo advertisement, *c.* 1949. John Yeo was a very well-known store in Plymouth, stocking a variety of fashions, fabrics and linens. After the war, both Spooner's and Yeo's moved to adjacent buildings on Royal Parade. Both buildings were later taken over by Debenham's department store.

Right: Advertisement for J. Dingle & Son, *c.* 1925. J. Dingle & Son were well-known butchers who were situated in Plymouth's market. After the Blitz, many major shops such as Woolworth's and Marks & Spencers were given stalls in the market so that they could carry on business as normal, while the smaller market traders opened stalls in Drake Street, commonly known as 'Tin Pan Alley'.

Royal Parade, *c.* 1954. More of Plymouth survived the bombing than people remember. Unfortunately, many of these buildings, though sound, were pulled down to make way for a new city centre. The new city's main feature was Royal Parade. Gone were the many old buildings which were replaced with modern, sleek, streamlined edifices.

Dingles, on the left, can be seen in this view of the recently built Royal Parade in the 1950s. When it opened, in September 1951, there was much excitement. It was the first large store to open in the country since the end of the war. On the far right of the picture is the John Yeo building.

two

People

Mr and Mrs Legg, c. 1920. Mr Legg, a corporal, served at the Royal Citadel looking after the horses. Work began on the Citadel in 1665 after Charles II recognised Plymouth's important position as a channel port. It incorporated an old fort built in the time of Sir Francis Drake. The cannons not only faced towards the sea but also towards the town. This was thought to have been to keep the town in order as it had supported the Parliamentarians during the Civil War in the reign of Charles' father, Charles I.

A studio photograph of Mr and Mrs Codd taken in Plymouth around 1900. Mr Codd sports a large Victorian moustache; these were very fashionable at the time. Although they both wear the typically dark dress of the day, this would probably have been their Sunday best and worn for special occassions like here, having their photograph taken.

The 2nd Battalion of the Devonshire Regiment, 1912. Shown here are the soldiers of No. 4 Section, 'F' Company at Stonehouse Barracks. The photographer is Easden of Plymouth. Stonehouse Barracks still stands at the beginning of Durnford Street. Royal Marines have been stationed here since the barracks' construction in 1783.

The marriage of William Cole to Elizabeth Stewart, 1940. From left to right: Betty Cole, Frederick Stewart, Bill (William) Cole, Betty (Elizabeth) Cole (*née* Stewart), Sidney Stewart and Kate Stewart. Mr and Mrs Cole ran the popular grocery shop at 144 King Street for many years.

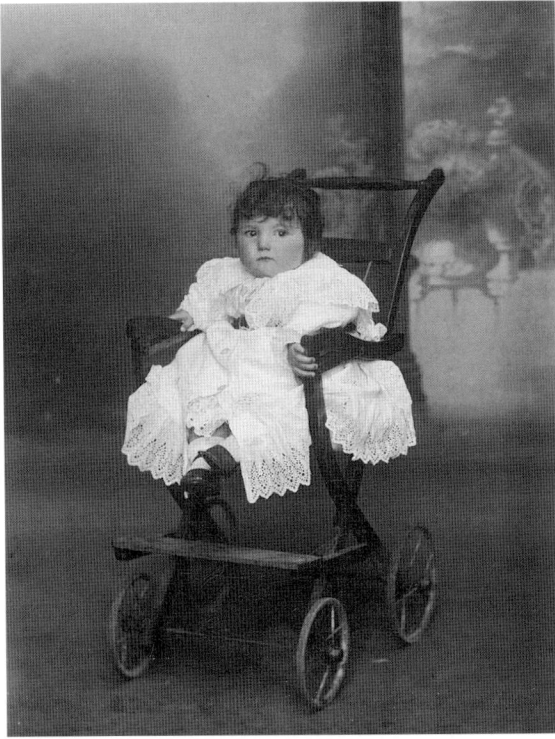

This shot of a baby in a very robust pram was taken at Elite Studios in Old Town Street in 1910. I bet she couldn't wait to get away! This contraption wouldn't have been like the comfortable prams of today and every cobble would have been felt by the sturdy rigid wheels.

Fairies, *c.* 1910. The National Union of Teachers, founded in 1869, held their annual conference in Plymouth in 1910 at the Guildhall and, with local children, performed a play called *Pixie Land*.

The marriage of Phyllis Bray and Ronald Rich, July 1933. From left to right, back row: Will Liddcoat, Harrold ?, Kathleen ?, Annabel ?, Auntie Mig, Uncle Fred, Mrs Burrows, Billy Murch. Middle row: Mary Dart, Edward Dart, Annie Dart, Granny Rich, Ethel ?, -?-, Marion ?, John Selleck, Grandad Bray. Front row: Arthur ?, Ronald Rich, Maurice Dart, Phyllis Bray, Myra ?.

The marriage of Mary Dart to Edward Dart, 17 February 1926. Mary and Edward Dart are featured in the middle of the picture and behind them, in hats, are the three bridesmaids, Dolly, Ivy and Elsie. The fashions – especially the cloche hats – really capture the period.

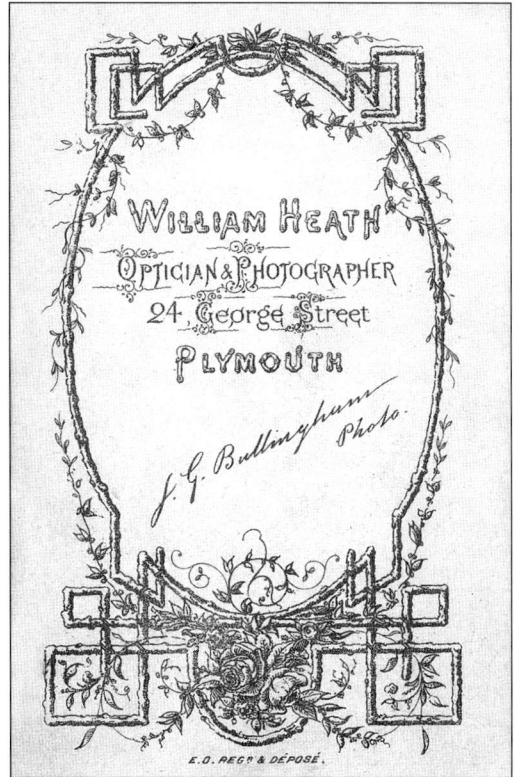

Carte de visite, c. 1900. Cartes de visite were small visiting card portraits and were introduced by André Disdéri in 1854. During the 1860s, there was a craze for these cards and one taken of Queen Victoria and Prince Albert sold over 100,000 copies. The picture on the left was taken in George Street, Plymouth, at William Heath studios, right, *c.* 1900. There were many photographic studios in Plymouth and William Heath owned one of the most popular. Located in George Street, he photographed many areas in and around Plymouth, some of which can still be found on old postcards.

Opposite above: The marriage of Annie Legg to George Gosling, 1923. It is interesting to see the fashions of the day. In the centre of the picture, with the large hat, is the bride, Annie Legg. To her left, with black hair, is the bridegroom, George Gosling, while on her right is Annie's grandfather, Mr Legg (first name unknown). From left to right, back row: –?–, Gladys Codd, –?–, Bessie Perry (*née* Legg), Harry Codd, Jack Legg. On the far left, holding his baby son Ken, is Richard Perry, whose wife Bessie is in the back row.

Opposite below: Salisbury Road School, 1931. Opened in the early twentieth century, the school originally had four sections: the main school, a part for deaf children, another part for 'defective' and epileptic children and finally a part for teacher-pupil instruction. During the First World War it was used as a hospital and in the Second as a billet for troops. Much of the school was destroyed by the Blitz and the special needs side of the school all but disappeared. Teachers there in the early days included Miss Angier, headmistress from 1903 to 1922, Miss Olivier from 1922 to 1942 and Pauline Membrey who had been a pupil at the school between 1928 and 1933 and returned as a teacher in 1950. Barbara Hill, with short bobbed hair, is immediately in front of the girl in white, standing at the back.

The marriage of Eric Webb to Barbara Hill, 19 February 1944. Barbara, a Plymouth girl, worked for E. Dingle's in Bedford Street and, during the war, joined the Women's Auxiliary Air Force. Eric worked for army intelligence in London. They first met on a train but it was another year before they saw each other again and married. Their honeymoon was spent in Richmond, Surrey in a basement with strangers sheltering from heavy enemy bombing. They were happily married for fifty-eight years.

The marriage of Phyllis Webb to Terry Collins. Eric Webb, in the pinstriped suit, is best man. The ceremony took place at the church of St Edward the Confessor at Home Park Avenue, Peverell. The original church was built in 1907 but the main part was built in 1935.

three

Entertainment

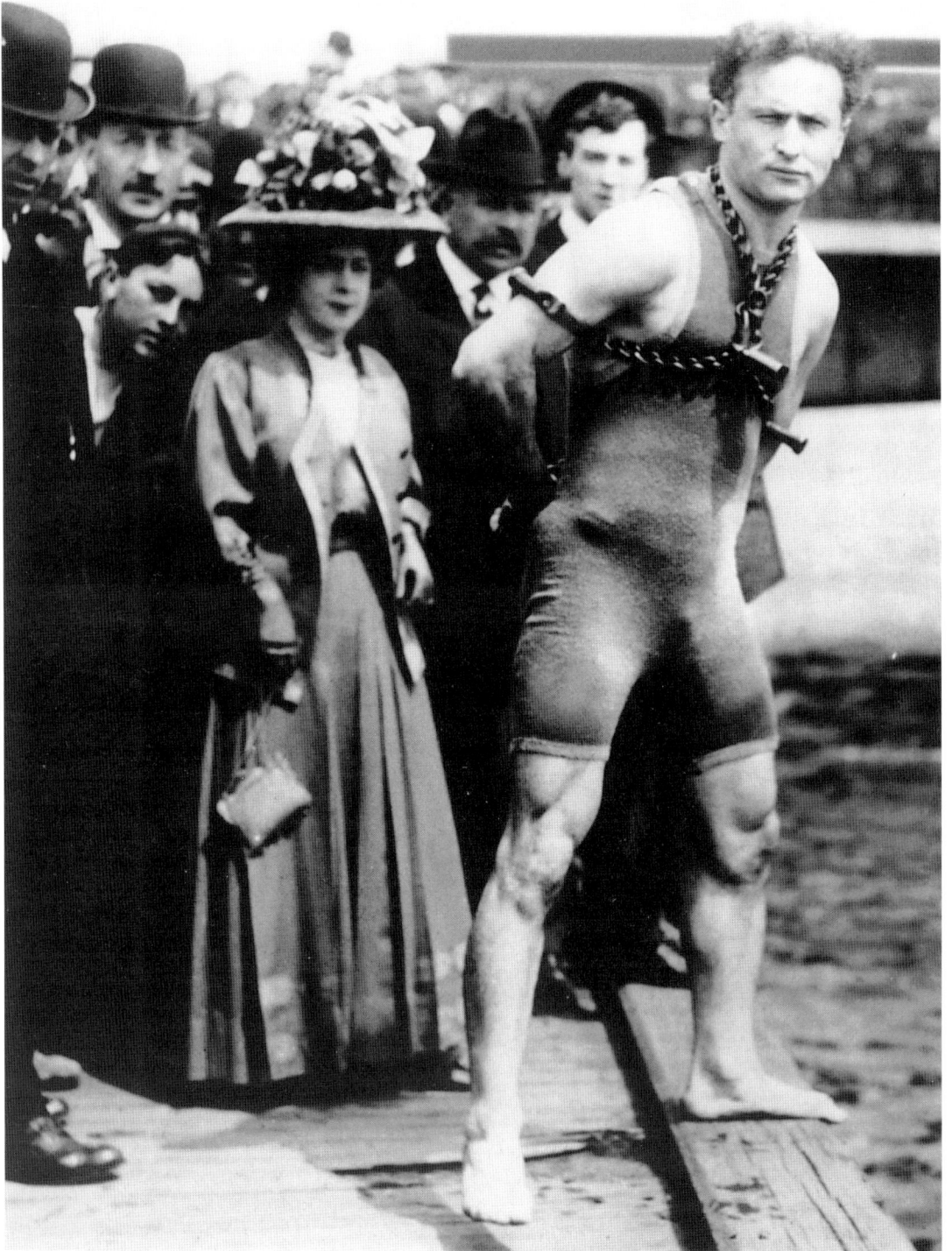

Harry Houdini, 1909. Houdini appeared at the Palace Theatre of Varieties during August 1909. There was much excitement at his appearance and he even challenged five joiners and mechanics at Devonport Dockyard to make a box from which he wouldn't be able to escape. They produced the box and Houdini was nailed inside. It took him twelve minutes to get out. Another of his daring feats involved him being securely handcuffed and diving from Halfpenny Bridge at Stonehouse. The story was covered in the *Western Morning News* of 18 August 1909 under the headline 'The Handcuff King':

Harry Houdini, the 'Handcuff King' who was performing at the Palace Theatre of Varieties, Plymouth, this week gave a remarkable exhibition of his skill yesterday afternoon at Stonehouse. The intrepid performer had previously announced his intention of diving from the Halfpenny Gate Bridge, securely handcuffed, and this caused a huge crowd to assemble on the bridge itself and on the adjoining quays and banks. Prompt to time Houdini appeared, stripped and poised himself on the parapet of the bridge. He was then handcuffed with his hands behind his back, while elbow locks were also worn, the chain passing around the neck. This accomplished, he immediately dived into the stream and disappeared from sight. Easily within the minute the 'Handcuff King' reappeared on the surface, carrying his fetters aloft in his right hand, while the crowd heartily cheered his exploit. Subsequently Houdini said that he had performed the diving trick over fifty times. He was capable of staying under water well over three minutes, but should he not appear in three minutes there were always ready two or three assistants who would swim to his rescue. The handcuffs and chains weighed 18lb.

The Theatre Royal and Atheneum, 1903. The Atheneum, built in the nineteenth century, had to be pulled down in the 1940s after German bombing. It was later rebuilt and was opened in May 1961 but without the classic Greek columns that had made it such a feature.

George Street, *c.* 1924. Gone are the horses and cabs that queued outside the Theatre Royal to take people home. Buses have appeared and they ran side by side with trams for many years to come. George Street featured a wide variety of shops including confectioners, tailors, hatters, watchmakers and even an umbrella-maker.

MONDAY, DEC. 10TH, 1900.

Theatre Royal,
PLYMOUTH.

The Three Towns' = =
= Amateur Operatic Society,

"LES CLOCHES DE CORNEVILLE,"

IN AID OF
THE ROYAL BRITISH FEMALE ORPHAN ASYLUM, STOKE,
AND THE
G. W. RAILWAY SERVANTS WIDOWS AND ORPHANS' FUND.

Doors open 7-15 p.m. Commence 7-30.
EARLY DOORS AT 7 (6D. EXTRA.)

C. F. WILLIAMS (Theatre Royal).
CHARLES JEFFERY (Hon. Conductor).

| ADMIT ONE. | |
| UPPER CIRCLE. | **2/-** |

A ticket for a performance of *Les Cloches de Corneville*, at the Theatre Royal, 1901. This and the ticket below were found in an old piano bought by Eric Webb that turned out to have woodworm and had to be taken apart. 'I never did learn to play the piano!' said Eric.

PUBLIC HALL, DEVONPORT.

Grand Special Performance

By ROYAL MARINE DRAMATIC COMPANY,

UNDER DISTINGUISHED PATRONAGE,

ON BEHALF OF THE
New Soldiers' and Sailors' Institute,

On THURSDAY, 7th MAY, 1903

"Black-Eyed Susan."

No. **35** **RESERVED SEATS, 2/-.**

Doors open at **7** p.m., Performance to
commence at **7-30** p.m. prompt.

H. L. SMITH, CLR.-SERGT., R.M.L.I
Stage and Business Manager.

A ticket for a performance of *Black-Eyed Susan* by the Royal Marine Dramatic Company, 1903. The marines not only played on the Hoe and in cafés in the city centre but regularly put on performances at Stonehouse Barracks, which housed the Globe Theatre, first used in 1820. The theatre had formerly been a racquet court and hayloft.

HOLLYWOOD'S GREATEST COMEDY COUPLE !

HERE IN PERSON

STAN

BERNARD DELFONT
presents

OLIVER

LAUREL AND HARDY

IN A NEW COMEDY MIRTHQUAKE "BIRDS OF A FEATHER"

Above: Laurel and Hardy theatre poster, 17 May 1954. Stan and Ollie were booked to play the last shows of their British tour at the Palace Theatre on 17 May 1954. The production was called *Birds of a Feather* and also playing on the same bill at the time were Harry Worth and 'Wonder Horse Tony'. Unfortunately, Oliver Hardy had a severe bout of flu and also suffered a mild heart attack and the show was cancelled. Ollie spent the rest of his stay in Plymouth recovering at the Grand Hotel on the Hoe.

Left: Laurel and Hardy, 1930s. The duo had visited Britain once before in 1932 when they were mobbed wherever they went. When they returned in 1954 they were handicapped by age and illness but still managed to give an exhausting thirteen shows a week.

Buffalo Bill, 3 June 1904.

Colonel W.F. Cody, known the world over as Buffalo Bill, gives two performances at Plymouth today in the course of his final tour of Great Britain with his unique exhibition of life in the Wild West. The location of the show at the Exhibition Fields, Pennycomequick, will make it readily accessible to residents of Plymouth, Devonport and Stonehouse, and special arrangements are being made by the railway companies to enable residents in outlying districts to witness the performance. No fewer than 800 horses participate in the show, and three special trains are employed to convey them and their properties from place to place. They arrived at Plymouth early this morning, and unloading, which occupied about two hours, began at 5.30. This show was patronised by thousands of people yesterday, on the occasion of its first visit to Bodmin. By the addition of a number of genuine Japanese soldiers to his Wild West Colonel Cody has acted only in response to a great public desire to see and learn something of these remarkable little men. Another new feature introduced is a daring leap through space by a cowboy on a bicycle. This rider starts from a height of 95 feet, and riding swiftly down an incline jumps from the incline across 40 feet of space to a continuing platform, and thence out of the arena. It is a most daring feat. The really big feature among the new things introduced by the colonel for his season, however is 'Custer's Last Stand' or 'The Battle of Little Big Horn'. In this over 300 men and horses participate, giving the most realistic representation of differing methods of warfare pursued by white and red man ever attempted, and making faithful representation of the massacre of Custer and 300 members of his regiment by a band of over 7,000 Indians led by the famous old chieftain Sitting Bull, whose only son, Willie Sitting Bull, is now a member of Colonel Cody's company, and is a daily participant in the mock battle. For the benefit of the country visitors, the Great Western Railway will run a late special train, which will leave Millbay at 10.55 p.m. calling at North Road and Mutley for Plymstock, Billacombe, Elburton Cross, Brixton Road, Steer Point and Yealmpton. (Extract from the *Western Morning News*)

Above left: Pier Pavilion advertisement, *c.* 1935. The Pier was popular with everyone for its concert parties, winter dances and even wrestling. The popular arcade had slot machines, chocolate machines and even a 'What the Butler Saw' hand-cranked machine.

Above right: Who's that girl? *c.* 1920. Does this photograph remind you of Tony Curtis in *Some Like it Hot*? That's because it's not what it first seems and features Edward Dart entering a fancy dress competition in the 1920s!

"OUR BOYS,"

ROYAL ALBERT HOSPITAL,

TUESDAY, 24th FEBRUARY, 1903.

ADMIT ONE.

Royal Albert Hospital, 1903. This ticket is for a performance of *Our Boys*. The Royal Albert Hospital, in Devonport, was founded in 1862. In 1918, electric lighting was installed with money raised by the nursing staff. It later became Plymouth General Hospital but was closed in 1981 when Derriford Hospital opened. The Royal Albert Hospital was demolished in 1982.

Plymouth Argyle, 1922. Back row: J. Devine, F. Cosgrove, J. Muir, W. Cook, P. Corcoran, W. Frost, J. Little, C. Miller. Second row: F. Haynes (trainer), I. Leathlean, J. Hill, J. Logan, R. Jack (secretary), J. Jobson, C. Eastwood, S. Atterbury (assistant trainer), A. Rhodes (assistant trainer). Seated: J. Dickinson, B. Bowler, H. Batten, H. Kirk, M. Russell, W. Forbes, H. Raymond, W. Baker, A. Rowe. Front row: J. Kirkpatrick, J. Fowler, J. Walker, T. Gallogley, F. Richardson, R. Jack, J. Leslie, A. Wilson.

Moses Russell, Plymouth Argyle, *c.* 1920s. Argyle played their first full game in 1886. Their captain was F. Howard Grose and the team would meet at Grose's home in Argyll Terrace. Originally called Argyle Athletic, they were named after Grose's admiration for the playing skills of the Argyll and Sutherland Highlanders regimental team. They originally only played away games as they had no pitch of their own and their practice sessions took place at Freedom Fields. In 1901 they started playing at the ground at Home Park, which had been built for the Devonport Albion Rugby Club. In the first two years, Home Park was also the home to whippet racing and cycling tournaments. In 1903 they were allowed to join the Southern League and played their first game as Plymouth Argyle.

Charabanc outing, *c.* 1920. Charabanc outings were very popular in the early decades of the twentieth century. This photograph shows an outing leaving from Plymouth. Popular destinations for outings included Mount Edgecumbe Park, Cawsands, Whitsands, Burrator and Saltash Passage. Huge crowds of people would leave Plymouth for these trips in large car-like vehicles. Many of these were works outings.

Right: Ida with bucket and spade, *c.* 1910. This photograph would have been taken on a day trip to the beach, possibly Whitsands or Cawsands. The beach was a popular destination for charabanc outings. It was not unusual for an outing to start at Cawsands and for the daytrippers to walk all the way to Mount Edgecumbe along the coast and through the park. There was a popular tea house in the grounds of Mount Edgecumbe park known as Lady Emma's Cottage and a lot of people would have met up there.

Below: Burrator reservoir, *c.* 1912. Work started on the dam in 1893 and it was officially opened by the Mayor, J.T. Bond, in 1898. The total cost was £178,000. The dams at Burrator and Sheepstor were raised by 10ft in 1923, which allowed the reservoir to hold a capacity of 1,026 million gallons. A suspension bridge was erected at the dam to carry works traffic and the remains can still be seen. This work was completed in 1928.

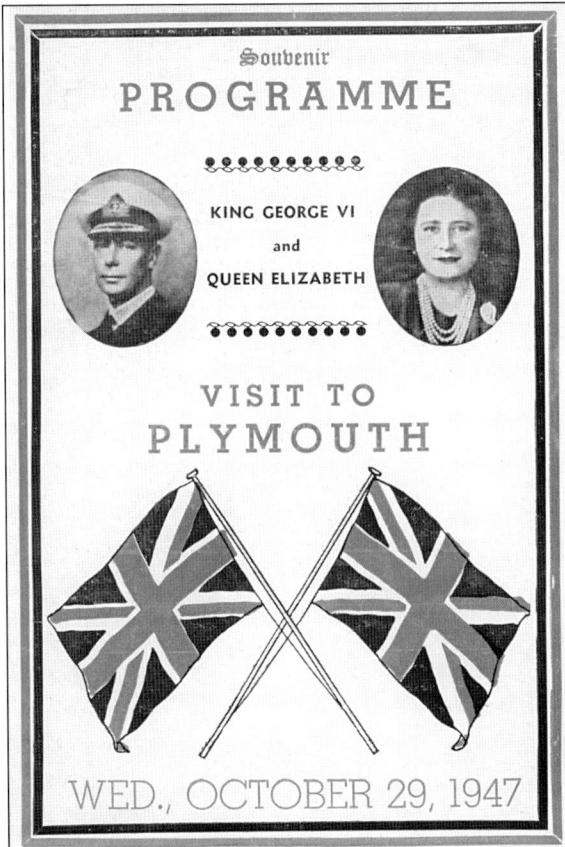

Above: Mount Edgecumbe park, *c.* 1905. The folly has always looked like this and isn't a ruin that has collapsed over the years. It was originally built in the early eighteenth century from the remains of two old Stonehouse chapels. An artist painting the scene at the end of the nineteenth century wrote that the Earl of Edgecumbe had his workers build one folly, had it blown up, didn't like the result and had it built and blown up again to get today's result.

Left: King George VI and Queen Elizabeth's visit to Plymouth, 29 October 1947. The King and Queen visited Plymouth to give a royal inauguration to the rebuilding of Plymouth's city centre which was destroyed by enemy action. Thousands of people turned out to see them. Royal Parade was built at a cost of £180,000. The western end of Royal Parade from Courtenay Street to Westwell Street was opened to coincide with the royal visit and the remaining part was completed on 27 September 1948.

four

Millbay Docks
and Laira Wharf

An aerial shot of Millbay Docks, 1930s. Built to plans by Isambard Kingdom Brunel, the dock cost a total of £250,000 and was completed in the 1840s. It was a major port until 1939 and sometimes received over 600 ocean liners a year.

RMS *Queen Mary*, 1930s. Plymothians would line the docks in the hope of seeing famous passengers disembark from the many ocean liners that stopped at Millbay Docks. The *Queen Mary* was Cunard's pride and joy. Famous passengers who docked at Plymouth on the *Queen Mary* included Gloria Swanson and Jack Warner, who both arrived in the city in 1938.

RMS *Mauretania*, 1930s. The *Mauretania* came to Plymouth regularly and delivered passengers and mail to the city. Film stars were quite often amongst the passengers, including the American crooner Bing Crosby. The *Mauretania* was built by Swan, Hunter & Wigham in Newcastle in 1907. It was the world's fastest liner from 1907 to 1927 and was part of Cunard Line's Liverpool to New York service.

Charlie Chaplin disembarked from the *Mauretania* in 1931 to the delight of many Plymothians who had come to see him. The star of many silent films, he made his famous film, *City Lights,* in that year. The *Mauretania* left on its final eastward crossing from New York to Southampton on September 1934, and was sent to the breakers' yard in July 1935.

The *Normandie*, *c.* 1937. The *Normandie* steamed into Plymouth Sound in 1937 after crossing the Atlantic in record-breaking time. The *Normandie* was the industry's first 1,000ft-long ocean liner. Walt Disney was among the many famous passengers who landed at Plymouth. The liner capsized and caught fire in New York while being converted for use in the Second World War. This picture of the liner was taken in Cawsand Bay just off Plymouth.

WHITE STAR LINER 'TITANIC.'
LEAVING SOUTHAMPTON DOCKS.
APRIL 10th 1912.

RMS *Titanic*, 1912. On 28 April 1912, the *Titanic* survivors were brought back to Millbay Docks, fourteen days after the ship had sunk. At 8.00 a.m., the SS *Lapland* moored at Cawsand Bay with the 167 members of the *Titanic* who had not been detained in New York for the American inquiry. Three tenders left Millbay Docks to collect the passengers and the 1,927 sacks of mail that had been scheduled to be carried by the Titanic. The third tender, the *Sir Richard Grenville*, carrying the survivors, killed time in the Sound while the dock labourers and porters were paid off and escorted out of the dock gates at West Hoe. After midday, the tender was given the all clear and the survivors were allowed to disembark in an air of secrecy. They were then put on a special train from Millbay Docks to Southampton where they arrived at 10.10 p.m. that night.

Opposite below: The *Lusitania*, c. 1910. The *Lusitania* was a regular visitor to Plymouth and would take emigrants all over the world. One trip in July 1878, bound for Adelaide, Australia, took over thirty-eight days. The *Lusitania* was torpedoed by a German U-boat in 1915 with the loss of 1,195 lives. The captain was thrown clear and survived the tragedy.

Millbay station, *c.* 1905. Liner passengers would start their journey to London from Millbay Station. Many film stars, including George Raft and Charlie Chaplin, would board the trains here with thousands of less famous travellers. Here, horses and cabs wait to take the passengers on to their hotels or next destination.

A ferryman, *c.* 1910. The great ocean liners would moor in the Sound or off Cawsand Bay and their passengers would be taken ashore by the ferrymen and their ferryboats, *Sir Richard Grenville* or *Sir Francis Drake*. The *Sir Richard Grenville* was built in 1931. It was the second ferryboat to be given this name, the original being built in 1891. Both were owned by the Great Western Railway, though in 1947 the second *Sir Richard Grenville* was transferred to the British Transport Commission. It was withdrawn from service in 1963.

Above: Loading clay at Laira Wharf, 1930s. Here, clay casks are being unloaded from wagons to be sorted and shipped worldwide. The first use of clay in the west of England was for the manufacture of porcelain. It is also now used in paint and cement, in the plastics and rubber industries and in various other products.

Right: Clay casks at Laira Wharf, 1930s. China clay has been worked on south-west Dartmoor since 1830. Many settlements at Lee Moor and Wotter exist only because of clay working. Arthur Bray can be seen in this picture. Notice how the track and wharf have been turned white by clay deposits.

Lee Moor tramway southbound, *c*. 1950. The Lee Moor tramway crossed the Great Western Railway line at Laira and, being an older route, the horse-drawn trucks took precedence over the trains. It was quite a journey from Lee Moor to Laira Wharf and the horses were well cared for and looked after as they would have to make this journey several times a day.

Trains loaded with clay wait to be sorted at Laira sidings, *c*. 1950. The eighteenth and nineteenth centuries saw a vast improvement in access to the moor with the development of tramways and railways. When china clay, or kaolin, was discovered in England, it was found to be of a far superior quality than its counterparts in Europe. William Cooksworthy initially discovered china clay at Tregonning Hill, near Helston, in 1746 and took out a patent in 1768 to use it for producing porcelain at his Plymouth factory.

Harry Osbourne and wagon at Laira Wharf, c. 1915. The china clay industry has been in existence for over 250 years and clay has been mined at Lee Moor for over 180 years. The clay at Lee Moor would be brought down to Laira Wharf by horse and cart to be loaded on to the many boats waiting there to take it worldwide.

End of Laira Junction, c. 1930. Here china clay is on its way from Lee Moor to Laira Wharf. There were sometimes up to a dozen trucks a day pulled by horses down to the wharf. Look at the boys' excitement to see the horses and trucks go by! The Lee Moor tramway was opened in 1858 but fell into disuse in 1939 and the track was taken up in 1961.

Left: Laira wharf, *c.* 1910. This photograph shows John Bray Junior and Captain Shelstroom, captain of a German clay boat. By 1910, almost a million tons of china clay a year were being produced and paper had become its prime use. Three-quarters of the output was shipped abroad to North America and Europe.

Below: Clay casks at Laira Wharf, 1930s. Clay production expanded greatly between 1950 and 1970 with a rising demand for clay from paper manufacturers worldwide. The value of clay sold to date, at today's prices, is a staggering £13.5 billion. For comparison, the amount of tin and copper sold works out to a total of about £9 billion.

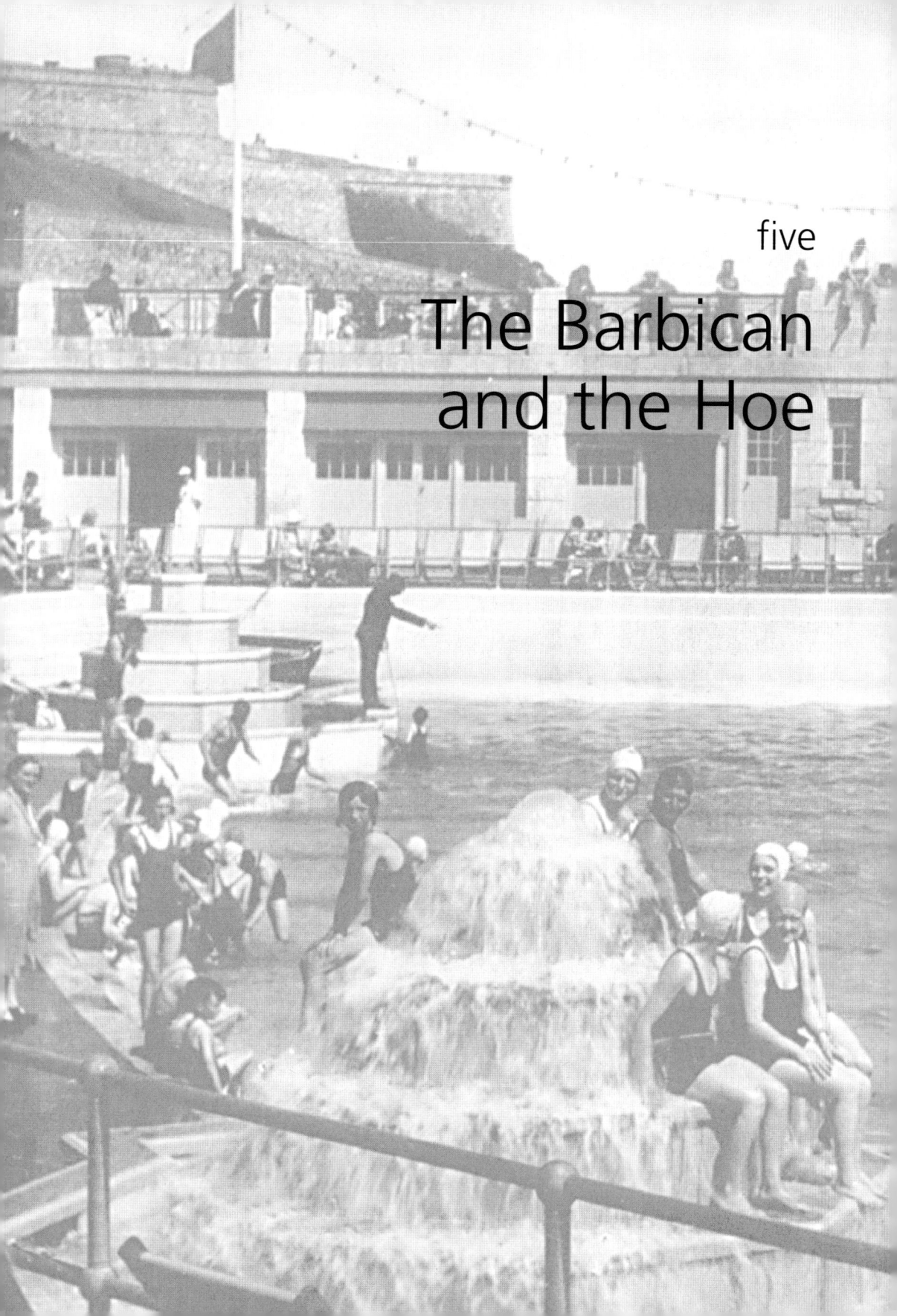

five

The Barbican and the Hoe

Sutton Harbour Fish Market, Plymouth

Sutton Harbour, *c.* 1910. The city of Plymouth had its origins around Sutton Harbour and the first dwellings of the town appeared here. Anglo-Saxon invaders landed here in AD 700; Sutton means 'south farm' in Old English. At the pool entrance there are two piers, built in 1791 and 1799, which were constructed to make the pool safe from tides.

Barbican fish quay, *c.* 1905. At the end of the nineteenth century, over 300 fishing boats could be seen in the harbour with 500 handcarts waiting for their catch. By 1890, more than 5,000 tons of fish would leave the area to be sent by rail.

The Barbican, *c.* 1905. In the foreground is the Mayflower Stone, the point from which the Pilgrim Fathers are said to have left Plymouth in 1620. However, at that time the water would have come much further back and the actual leaving point is said to be where the ladies' toilets stand in the Admiral McBride public house. Try telling that to an American tourist!

The Barbican, 1930s. The Barbican was originally known as Watergate and was once part of a castle that defended the entrance to Sutton Pool. All that now remains of the original castle is part of a wall at Lambhay Street.

New Street, c. 1920. The Elizabethan House in New Street dates from 1584 and is a restored captain's dwelling. It's not hard to imagine Walter Raleigh, Francis Drake, John Hawkins or Captain Cook wandering down the narrow cobbled streets here.

Mayflower memorial, c. 1940. The memorial and canopy were built in 1934 to commemorate the sailing of the Pilgrim Fathers to the New World. It was designed by J. Wibberley at a cost of £239. The memorial tablet dates from 1891.

The pier, *c.* 1887. The pier was opened in 1884 and cost £45,000 to build. It attracted huge crowds who came either to take a stroll on its decks or to attend dances or concerts. There were also regular skating sessions and boxing in the pavilion. It was destroyed in the Blitz of 1941 and the last remains of it were removed in 1953.

Interior of the pier, *c.* 1905. All manner of shows were held at the pier. In the winter there were regular concerts and in the summer there was wrestling, dancing and performances on Sundays by the Royal Marines band.

GRAND HOTEL THE HOE

DIRECTLY FACING THE SEA　　FULLY LICENSED

★

COCKTAIL LOUNGE

Telephone: 4393

100 Bedrooms, all with running Hot and Cold Water.　Private Suites.　Lift. Electric Fires for Bedrooms.　Lounges with open fires.　Sun Terrace Enclosed.　Lockup Garages.　　　R.A.C. and A.A. Gentlemen's Hairdressing Saloon. Open All the Year Round for Luncheon, Tea and Dinner

Tariff and further details from P. G. H. LANGFORD, *Manager*

PROPRIETORS: HEATHS (PLYMOUTH) LTD.

The Grand Hotel, *c.* 1950. The hotel was built by John Pethick in 1879 and he also became the first owner. At the time, the Grand was the only hotel in Plymouth with a sea view and advertisements stated that it had the finest view in Europe.

Opposite below: The Bowling Green, *c.* 1910. Francis Drake is said to have spotted the Spanish Armada from here whilst playing bowls. However, the site of the Green at that time would have been a lot further back, somewhere near to where the ABC cinema stands today.

The Esplanade, 1950s. This view of the Esplanade has been taken from the Grand Hotel. In the foreground you can see a few early cars. In the background is the Citadel and also the aquarium with views stretching towards Mount Batten. Note that Smeaton's Tower was painted white at the time. It has now been painted in its original red and white striped paint scheme but has endured some ghastly colours over the years!

Plymouth Hoe, 1930s. The Hoe is dominated by Smeaton's Tower, which lit the Channel fifteen miles off Plymouth's shore for 123 years before it was transferred to its current site. It has been a landmark on Plymouth Hoe for over 100 years and attracts thousands of visitors.

The Marines Band playing on the Hoe, *c.* 1905. Huge crowds would gather to hear the band play on the Hoe. The bandstand was hit by a bomb during the Second World War and unfortunately was never replaced.

Drake's Statue, 1920s. Drake looks out to the Sound to see the invading Armada from probably the best vantage point he's ever had! The statue is a duplicate of the one that stands on the approach to Tavistock, Drake's birthplace.

The Marines Band on the Hoe, c. 1905. This early scene shows the bandstand in the middle of the picture. To the right is a building very often thought to be the old camera obscura. However, the actual obscura building was based further back along the Esplanade just above the Belvedere. People would form large queues at the obscura to see the spectacular all-round view that was projected there. It lasted from about 1860 to 1890.

Above: The pier, *c.* 1887. The pier was officially opened on 25 May 1884. The mayor, John Greenway, was presented with a silver gilt key to unlock the gate. About 30,000 people attended the ceremony of which 10,000 were on the pier. Unfortunately, by 1922 interest in the pier had waned and some of the passenger steamers that cruised the Sound and the Tamar were sold off. By 1938, after continuing losses, the receiver was called in and there were discussions about what to do with the pier. An attempt to sell it to the City Council failed but the problem was 'solved' by the Blitz of 1941.

Left: The foundation stone for the Armada Memorial was laid in 1888, on the 300th anniversary of the first sighting of the Spanish Armada. The statue at the top of the pedestal is a bronze figure of Britannia. It was unveiled on 21 October 1890 by the then Duke of Edinburgh.

Hoe Slopes, *c.* 1910. The scene looks much the same today except for the tram following the road, probably stopping at the pier. It's interesting to see the children of the time sitting on the bank, most are wearing hats.

BATHING POOL, THE HOE, PLYMOUTH.

Men's pool, 1920s. In 1860, all-day swimming was allowed but, as was reported in the local newspaper, 'dead cats and sewerage spoiled it'. In 1877, a ladies' pool was opened west of Tinside and in 1907, a men's pool opened adjacent to the pier. In 1919, mixed bathing was allowed.

The Lido at Tinside. The pool was opened on 2 October 1935. It was an important occasion and thousands of people turned up to witness the event. At the time, the art deco pool was a spectacular sight with three fountains to aerate the water and, at night, floodlighting from below.

The Lido, c. 1938. The Lido has been a popular attraction for adults and children for many years. Although it was allowed to fall into disrepair in recent times, it has now been refurbished and is ready to welcome many future generations.

Boats in the Sound, *c.* 1910. This view, taken from the pier, shows the many small boats that occupied the Sound at the time. The Sound was a busy place for sailing craft. Many fishing boats would leave from the Barbican and pass this way. There would also be pleasure boats, ocean liners and Navy warships occupying the waters.

Drake's Statue, *c.* 1910. The statue was unveilled by Lady Elliot Drake, a descendant of Drake, in front of 20,000 people on 14 February 1884. The day was observed in the three towns as a holiday. The sculptor was criticised, though, for making Drake too handsome and too tall and for more resembling Drake's friend, Sir John Hawkins.

The Hoe Slopes, 1940s. 'Hoe' is the Old English word for 'high place'. This shot shows the pier and, on the road, cars have replaced horses and carts. The trams have now gone to be replaced by buses.

The Esplanade, Plymouth Hoe

The Esplanade, c. 1915. This view, taken from near to the aquarium, stretches over the Esplanade to West Hoe in the background. Smeaton's Tower and the bandstand are on the left and the Armada memorial is on the right.

The Hoe Slopes, *c.* 1910. Notice the man wearing a boater with his two little girls, probably on their way to stroll the boards or to play the arcade machines on the pier. The foreshore was developed in 1913.

An excellent pre-Blitz view of the city from Smeaton's Tower, *c.* 1920. The Guildhall and St Andrew's Church are easily visible. The monument is the Armada Memorial, designed by Herbert Gribble of London, and incorporating a bust of Sir Francis Drake with the inscription 'England expects that every man will do his duty'.

View from West Hoe towards the Hoe, *c.* 1905. A pleasure boat can be seen leaving the jetty, probably for a trip up the River Tamar. The Citadel is in the background. This photograph also gives a good side view of the pier stretching out into the Sound.

Crowds line the top of the Hoe at the bathing place for the Plymouth Regatta, *c.* 1910. The Regatta was held annually and would draw thousands of people to the Hoe. Regular swimming contests on the Hoe would also draw large crowds.

Right: Eddystone Lighthouse, *c.* 1910. This was the fourth Eddystone lighthouse to be built. The first two had been constructed of wood. The first, built in 1698, was washed out to sea taking its architect, Winstanley, with it. The second, built by Rudyerd in 1706, caught fire and was destroyed. John Smeaton began work on the third lighthouse, to be built completely from stone, in 1756. When the Eddystone lighthouse was replaced by James Douglass in 1877, Smeaton's Tower was removed block by block and rebuilt on the Hoe. The stump where Smeaton's Tower once stood can still be seen alongside the current lighthouse.

Below: Plymouth Sound, *c.* 1905. Not too much has changed in this view since Sir Francis Drake's time though the Sound has seen many nautical events since, such as Sir Francis Chichester returning home from his round the world voyage in 1967.

EDDYSTONE LIGHTHOUSE.

Left: Citadel Gate, *c.* 1920. Built in 1670, the gate still stands today. There was once a drawbridge and a moat but these were filled in in 1888. There was also a statue of Charles II where the cannonballs now stand.

Below: Plymouth from the Citadel, *c.* 1910. In the foreground is the South African War Memorial. It was unveilled on 8 August 1903 by Lady Audrey Buller and commemorates the soldiers who fell during the Boer War of 1899-1902.

six

Transport

Car no. 4, at the Stonehouse end of Union Street, *c.* 1910. This tram belonged to the Plymouth, Stonehouse & Devonport Tramways, a company that ran between 1901 and 1922. At the time, they had a fleet of sixteen electric trams. This one is brightly decorated with advertisements, including one for the *Western Morning News*.

Opposite above: Car no. 15 in St Levan's Road, Devonport, with the gasometers behind, *c.* 1909. While Plymouth, Devonport and Stonehouse were still three separate entities, the three towns first tramway was opened in 1872. It ran from Derry's Clock in Plymouth, through Union Street, across Stonehouse toll bridge and as far as Cumberland Gardens in Devonport.

Opposite below: Devonport and district tram built by Brill, 1929. This tram was a 'special' and its destination is given as 'Football'. Argyle would have been playing at home. It is pictured at Milehouse on its way to Fore Street. In the background, the Britannia public house is just visible.

Left: Tram at Stonehouse, *c.* 1930. Part of the Plymouth Corporation Tramways, this tram's destination would have been 'Theatre' via Union Street from Devonport, one of the most used lines in Plymouth. On its side are its destinations including North Road and Fore Street. This one features an advertisement for Jacob's Crackers.

Above right: A Plymouth Corporation token to be used on the trams or buses. This one is for 1d and would have been used sometime in the late 1920s. Trams had run by various means. The best known were horse-drawn trams and the later electric ones. However, in 1882, the Plymouth, Devonport & District Tramways Company wanted to build an extensive steam tramway system. The borough of Devonport objected to the lines being open and run in Plymouth before they had been completed in Devonport. A service started on 3 November 1884 but ended on the 14th after the Devonport Corporation obtained an injuction to halt the service.

Opposite above: No. 34 tram at Durnford Street, *c.* 1928. You wait all day for a tram and five come at once! Durnford Street is steeped in history. Sir Arthur Conan Doyle assisted at a medical practice here and Sherlock Holmes was said to be based on his colleague, Dr Budd.

Opposite below: No. 119 tram at Milehouse depot, 1930s. This tram's destination would have been Fore Street via Peverell. A member of the Plymouth Corporation Tramways fleet, these were beautifully decorated. This one carried advertisements for Masons OK sauce and *Punch*.

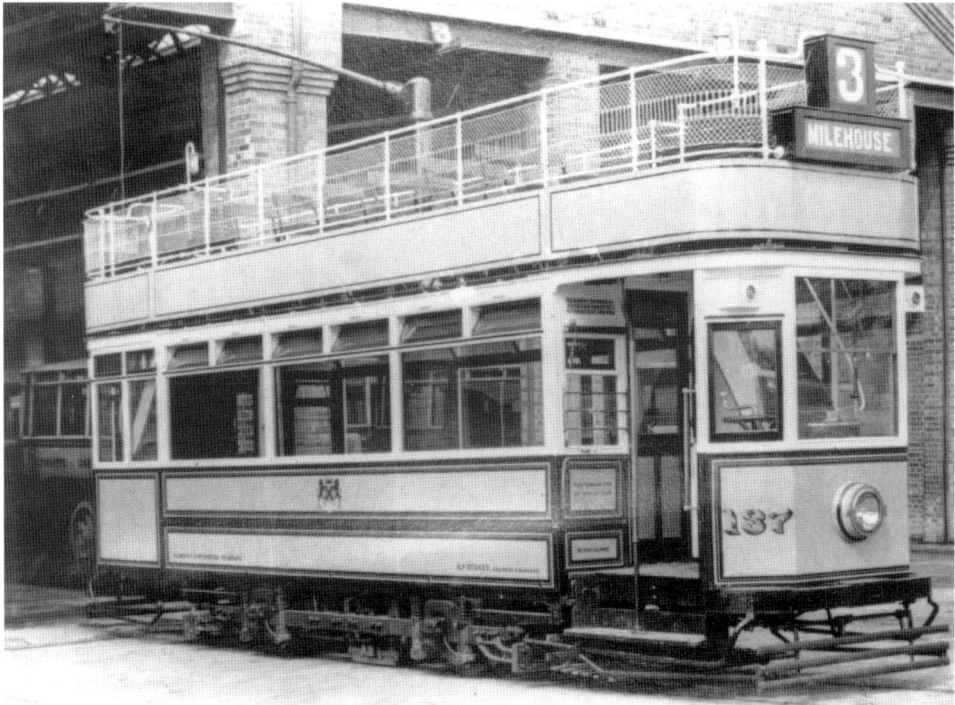

No. 137 tram at Milehouse Depot, *c.* 1938. Known as a 'Squareface' model, this tram would have been painted in yellow. It is pictured at the back of Milehouse sheds. Trams suffered a lot of wear and tear and had to be maintained regularly. They also had to be updated to comply with the strict safety regulations of the time.

No. 12 tram at Peverell tramway terminus, *c.* 1909. This tram is travelling down Peverell Park Road towards the Royal Theatre. A horse and buggy follow very close behind, probably heading for the same destination. It wasn't until 1899 that the Tramways Department opened its first electric tram service. On the left of this picture is the Plymouth Mutual Co-operative and Industrial Society building.

Trams at Mutley Plain, *c.* 1909. The tram at the front is the no. 19 and would have been part of the Plymouth, Stonehouse & Devonport Tramways fleet. It has an advertisement for Fry's Cocoa on the side. On the right of the picture is the Plymouth Mutual Co-operative Society building.

A tram heading towards Peverell, *c.* 1927. This tram was one of fifteen built by the Plymouth Corporation Tramways Department at Milehouse Depot in 1927 and 1928. They were built of teak as the manager thought they would look better as varnished wood rather than being painted over. Most of these trams lasted until 1945.

Mutley train station, *c.* 1910. Mutley station opened in 1849 and was closed in 1939. Some of the old buildings in the background are still very recognisable today. Mutley would have been a busy station as a stop-off point for the many shops and businesses on Mutley Plain and also for Plymouth College and several other schools and churches in the area.

Plympton station, *c.* 1910. A stationmaster waits for the next train to arrive. In 1904, the Great Western Railway started a new service between Saltash and Plympton. The same year also saw halts opened at Laira and Lipson Vale and platforms were put in at St Budeaux and Ford.

Duke of Cornwall Hotel, *c.* 1910. Built in 1865 by John Pethrick, the Duke of Cornwall Hotel catered for passengers from the nearby Millbay station either en route to London or travelling abroad via Millbay Docks.

Right: Duke of Cornwall Hotel advertisement, 1930s. The Duke of Cornwall Hotel advertised itself as, 'the recognised Hotel for ocean passengers', many of whom disembarked from the great ocean liners that landed at Millbay Docks.

Duke of Cornwall Hotel

Telegrams— "Dukotel"   **PLYMOUTH**   Telephone— 735

A.A.   FIRST-CLASS HOTEL   R.A.C.

PROVIDED WITH EVERY MODERN CONVENIENCE.

Recognised Hotel for Ocean Passengers. Near Docks, Hoe and G.W. Railway Station.

MODERATE CHARGES.

Bedrooms with Private Baths and H. & C. water. Central Heating. Lift to all Floors. Inclusive Terms.

Apply for Tariff to **MANAGER**.

CONTINENTAL HOTEL

About half a mile from North Road Station (close to Millbay, now used only for goods) and convenient for most points
of interest. Hot and cold water and gas fires in bedrooms

LARGE GARAGE   **TELEPHONE 342311**

TRUST HOUSES LIMITED

Continental Hotel, 1940s. The late nineteenth century saw a lot of
activity at Millbay Docks and the Great Western Railway Company
decided to build their Plymouth terminal nearby. With a large
amount of passengers arriving at the station, it was decided to build a
number of hotels to accomodate them. In 1875, the Albion Hotel
opened its doors. The Albion adjoined the Royal Eye Infirmary but
this was later taken over by the owner of the Albion, George Fowler,
and renamed Fowler's Hotel. By 1904, the two businesses had
become collectively known as the Albion and Continental Hotels.

Plympton station, *c.* 1910. A maintenance team pose for the camera. Plympton station was opened in 1848 by the South Devon Railway and closed in 1959. The houses that can be seen in the background still stand today.

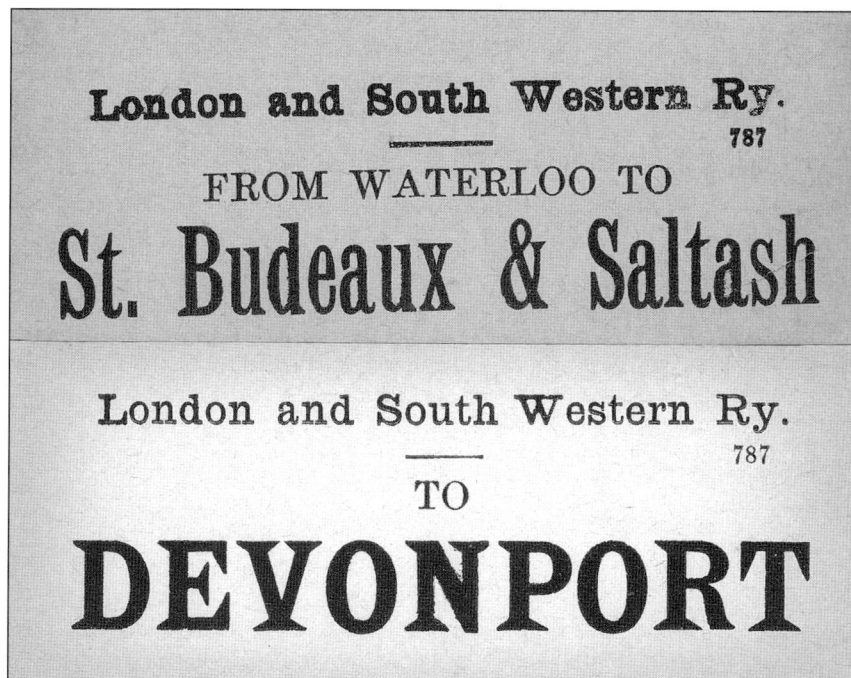

These labels date from the 1920s and would have been attached to the luggage of passengers travelling to the busy stations of Devonport and St Budeaux and to Saltash in Cornwall.

Millbay station, *c.* 1905. The tracks ran from Millbay station straight into the docks. As well as VIPs, the trains carried various cargoes from ships, including gold bars and spices. Built in 1849, it was nicknamed the 'Shabby Shed'. Millbay station closed in 1941 after bombing and the platform lines were used solely for goods traffic. In 1966, the line was closed to public goods traffic and finally, in 1971, the last track into Millbay Docks was closed.

Devonport station, *c.* 1910. Devonport station stood in King's Road where the College of Further Education now stands. Known as King's Road station, the platforms were lit by gas lanterns. Many dockyard workers used the station and farm produce would arrive there to be taken to the nearby Devonport market.

Millbay station, *c.* 1910. A popular excursion leaving Millbay station was the sixpenny Woolworth trains heading for Dartmoor. These would be so packed at times that passengers would be turned away. Evening trips would run to Newquay and St Ives. The site of the station is now occupied by the Plymouth Pavilions, an entertainment centre.

Mutley station, *c.* 1912. A slope led down to the station and a cab would wait at the top to drop off or collect passengers. On Sundays at 4.30 p.m., daytrippers could catch one of the 'special' trains from Mutley station bound for Shaugh Bridge, Clearbrook and Yelverton.

Plymstock station, *c.* 1910. A young boy waits with a trolley to unload the passengers' baggage. At one time, sixty trains passed by here every day on their way to Turnchapel or Yealmpton.

Plymstock platform, *c.* 1915. A stationmaster has a quick smoke and chat with the train driver. By 1930, passenger numbers had dwindled and the station remained open for freight only until 1960.

Opposite above: Lee Moor tramway crossing being relaid at Laira junction, 1930s. Regular maintanance had to be carried out on the lines, which were in constant use from trains and trams. At a time when there were few or no cars, everybody would travel by rail.

Opposite below: Empty wagons at Laira yard, 1940s. These empty wagons would be waiting to transport goods and produce across the region. These ones would probably have been used to transport china clay from Lee Moor to the docks at Laira Wharf.

Laira Halt, *c.* 1905. A busy platform scene as commuters hurry to get on the train. Everyone seems to be dressed-up for the occassion – notice the young boys in their neat suits and white collars and the ladies in their large hats with bows on.

Ford station, *c.* 1910. Ford station was opened on 2 June 1890 by the Plymouth, Devonport & South Western Junction Railway. It was closed on 7 September 1964 and a housing estate now stands in its place. Notice the Edwardian gent on the left.

Tamerton Foliot station, *c.* 1912. Now long since gone, the station at the time would have been considered as being out in the country. It can still be found at the end of a nature reserve but it has been a private house for many years now. If you stand on the bridge today and look over, it really hasn't changed much.

A steam train pulls into Plympton station, *c.* 1908. The Great Western Railway, which had run many of the lines in Plymouth and the surrounding area, ceased to exist on 31 December 1947 and the system became the Western Region of British Railways.

Keyham station, *c.* 1910. Keyham station was opened on 1 July 1900 by the Great Western Railway. The station is still open but became unmanned in 1969. It was a well-used route for dockyard workers and sailors. The tin shed on the right is a waiting room and an old sign advertises 'Titleys'.

Stonehouse Pool station, *c.* 1910. Devonport and Stonehouse station was opened in 1876. A branch line led down to the Stonehouse Quay terminus. In the early twentieth century, passengers would arrive here by tender from the great ocean liners to be taken by railway to London. The sign reads 'South Western Railway Ocean Quay Station'. An armaments factory was also situated nearby and, during the First World War, troops would land here.

Opposite below: St Budeaux station, 1930s. From St Budeaux station you could catch a train to Saltash over the Royal Albert Bridge and be in Cornwall within minutes. For many years, this was the main route to Cornwall for travellers. The station opened on 2 June 1890 and the Revd William Green, the local vicar, arranged for the church bells to be rung in celebration. The station was built by the Plymouth, Devonport & South West Junction Railway.

St Budeaux station, 1930s. This was a popular station that serviced the ever-growing area of St Budeaux; it was used frequently by sailors and dockyard workers. It was also used by the many travellers who came to visit the picturesque Saltash Passage. When it first opened, the stationmaster was a Mr Edmund Tolley who lived in walking distance of the station.

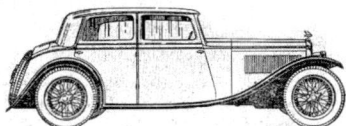

Above: Torpoint Ferry, *c.* 1910. The ferry first began its service in 1791 and was mainly used to bring the ever-growing workforce to Devonport Dockyard. The fares were 1d for foot passengers, 2d for horses and 1s 6d for a horse and cart.

Left: Advertisement for Mumford's, *c.* 1933. Mumford's is probably one of the city's best-known garages. W. Mumford Ltd was founded in 1900 and the company has been servicing cars in the city ever since. Mumford's have adapted greatly to deal with the many changes to automobiles over the last hundred or so years.

Torpoint Ferry, 1940s. In 1834, James Rendel introduced a chain ferry to the crossing. Previously the ferry had been attached to rowing boats and later, in 1828, a short-lived steamboat had been introduced. The ferry became the property of Cornwall County Council in 1922.

Plymouth double-decker bus, with its driver and two conductors, c. 1949. Notice how this bus has a crank to get it started. By 1922, motor buses were running in the city and trams became a less viable proposition. In 1941, only the line from Drake's Circus to Peverell still ran with trams but this was discontinued after the war and the city's last tram ran on 29 September 1945.

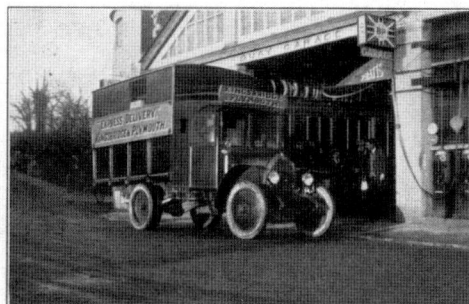

"EXPRESS DELIVERY."

KINGSBRIDGE AND PLYMOUTH

VIA

CHURCHSTOW   AVETON GIFFORD   MODBURY   YEALMPTON

TORQUAY
Every FRIDAY
Leave
Kingsbridge
about 9.30 a.m.
Torquay about 4 p.m.
via. Totnes and Paignton.

Van available
for other Trips
Mondays
and
Wednesdays

TUESDAYS, THURSDAYS, SATURDAYS

Leave KINGSBRIDGE about   9 a.m. (Quay)
„   PLYMOUTH   „   3.30 p.m. (Norley Yard)

We shall be pleased to convey Passengers and any class of Goods to and from Plymouth.

We give every care and attention to all Goods entrusted to us and our charges are moderate.

Parcels may be left at our Office in **MILL STREET** or our Van will call if we are notified.

We solicit your Orders, which shall have our prompt and careful attention.

A. BURGOYNE, :: MILL STREET, KINGSBRIDGE

A poster advertising A. Burgoyne's express delivery service between Kingsbridge and Plymouth in the 1930s. Burgoyne vans and lorries were a common site in Plymouth. Not only did they convey passengers and goods to and from Plymouth, but they also were responsible for transporting stone, coal and fertiliser from Plymouth's docks.

Opposite below: Double-decker bus, *c.* 1947. Amazingly, this is the Royal Parade after both the Blitz and the war but before the new development took place. Some buildings still stand in the picture but these were later cleared to make way for the city-centre buildings that we see today.

Burgoyne's fleet, 1936. The Burgoyne vehicles were regularly seen in Plymouth, especially during the war when they helped clear up the debris from bombing in Devonport and Stonehouse. Huge areas of bomb damage existed in Plymouth and large areas, such as the open space opposite King Street, were not developed until the late 1980s.

Alfred Burgoyne's traction engine, 1923. The engine was bought new in 1920. On the far right is Bill Elliott, the driver, and next to him are Alfred Burgoyne (proprietor) and Christopher Thomas (lead man in goods yard). The engine features original storage tanks from the BP station at Kingsbridge. The truck later had sides and was used for conveying stones back and forth from Plymouth.

seven

Devonport and the Dockyard

ROYAL NAVAL BARRACKS GATE, KEYHAM. DEVONPORT

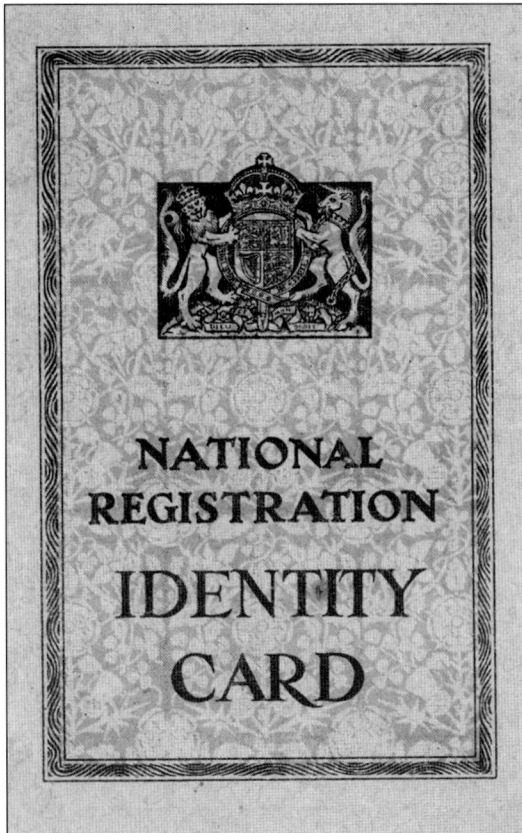

NATIONAL
REGISTRATION
IDENTITY
CARD

Above: Naval Barracks, Keyham, *c.* 1920. This view is still recognisable today as the entrance to HMS *Drake*. Built of Portland stone, the original buildings from the nineteenth century included two accommodation blocks, a drill shed and a dwelling for the Commodore.

Left: National Registration Identity Card, 1939. National registration was introduced in September 1939 and, during wartime, everyone was issued with a card that they had to carry at all times. This one was issued for a Civil Defence Warden working in the dockyard.

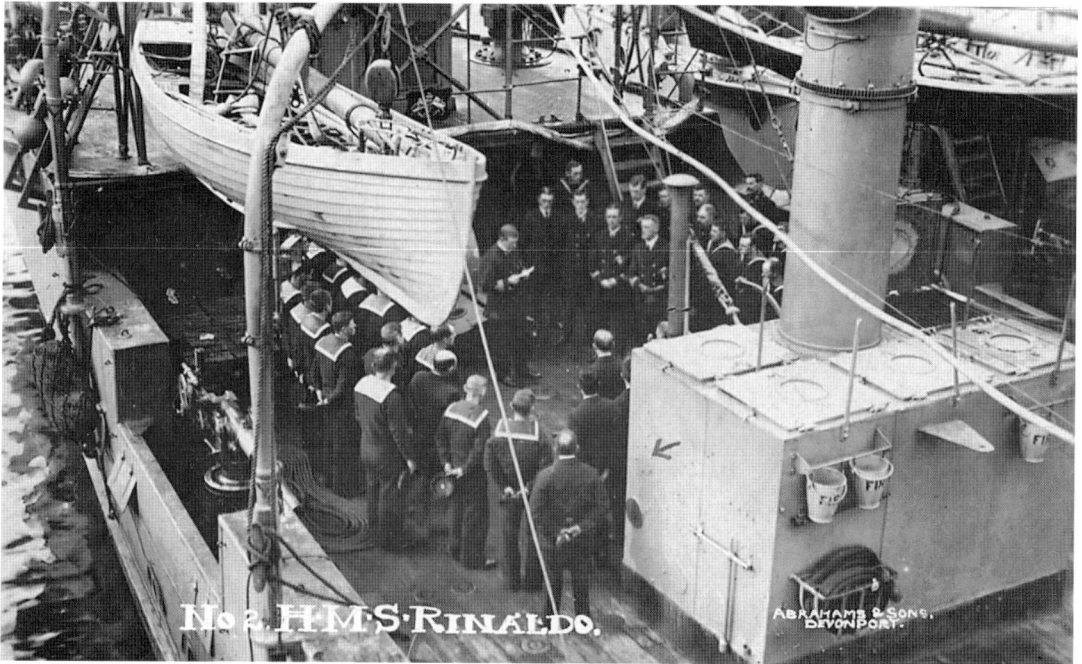

A service being held on board HMS *Rinaldo* at Devonport Dockyard, 1917. HMS *Rinaldo* was a Condor-class sloop launched in 1899. It was sold for scrap in 1921. This is one of the many naval ships that have carried the name HMS *Rinaldo* over the years.

Royal Naval Barracks, *c.* 1920. Work was started on the Royal Naval Barracks at Keyham in 1880. The total project cost £250,000 and the buildings could accommodate 5,000 men. The clock tower was completed on 20 May 1896.

Edward Dart planing in the dockyard, 1920s. The first dockyard was built on the Hamoaze on the banks of the River Tamar in the late seventeenth and early eighteenth centuries. By 1712, there were 318 men employed there and, by 1733, over 3,000 people were employed. The dockyard underwent major expansion in the late eighteenth century and the early nineteenth century as a result of the war with France.

Devonport Park, *c.* 1908. Devonport Park was built in 1858. Seen here at the entrance to the park in Stoke Road is the Swiss Lodge, which was designed by Alfred Norman of Devonport. In the 1860s, the park was rented by Devonport from the War Office for a yearly sum of £65.

Devonport Park, *c.* 1910. Devonport Park stretches for 37 acres. Originally, there was a bandstand in the park which, in the summer, would be visited by local regiments and volunteers who would entertain the public.

Above: An early etching of Devonport Gardens showing the Swiss Lodge and the main fountain, *c.* 1887. The park was later extended and improved in 1894. The main walk follows an old trench that use to surround Granby Barracks.

Left: Edward Dart on his allotment in Stoke, 1939: Allotments played a vital part in food production during the Second World War. Between the wars, there had been a drop-off in interest in allotments and much of the land was used for houses.

College of Engineering, *c*. 1910. The college opened on 1 July 1880 as a training school for engineering students. It was occupied by 120 students who were given board and lodging. They would spend five years there before being drafted onto sea-going vessels as assistant engineers.

Devonport Technical School, seen here around 1910, was opened on 25 July 1899 by the Mayor, W. Hornbrook. Technical schools were unheard of before the nineteenth century. Until 1936, Devonport Technical housed the Devonport Municipal Secondary School for Girls (Devonport High School for Girls).

Keyham Steam Yard, *c.* 1877. In the 1830s, a quarter of the Navy's vessels were powered by steam and a new yard was built to service them. Work started in 1845 and the site occupied 72 acres. The total cost of the project was £1,333,000. In October 1853, Queen Mary attended the opening of the Keyham Steam Yard extension.

Advertisement for the Royal Hotel, *c.* 1931. The Royal Hotel at Devonport boasted that it was the oldest established hotel in the city and dated from the eighteenth century. It had sixty bedrooms and catered mainly for military personnel.

Opposite below: Mount Wise, *c.* 1912. Sir Thomas Wise owned the Manor of Stoke Damerell and had a manor house at Keyham. When Mount Edgecumbe house was built in 1547, Sir Thomas decided to build a Tudor dwelling looking out to sea, which he named Mount Wise. Today, the maritime headquarters at Mount Wise serves as a Naval Reserve training centre known more commonly in the Royal Navy as HMS *Vivid*. It was formally commissioned in 1959. The unit has a total of 250 reservists.

Left: Lieutenant William Lockwood Lang of the 30th Corps Royal Engineers motorcycle division stationed at Mount Wise, March 1915.

Below: Mount Wise, 1890s. Mount Wise consisted of twenty-one detached buildings. It included workshops for many trades including joiners, smiths and harness-makers all employed to build up stores for military use. The officers' houses stood on the eastern side.

eight

The Outskirts

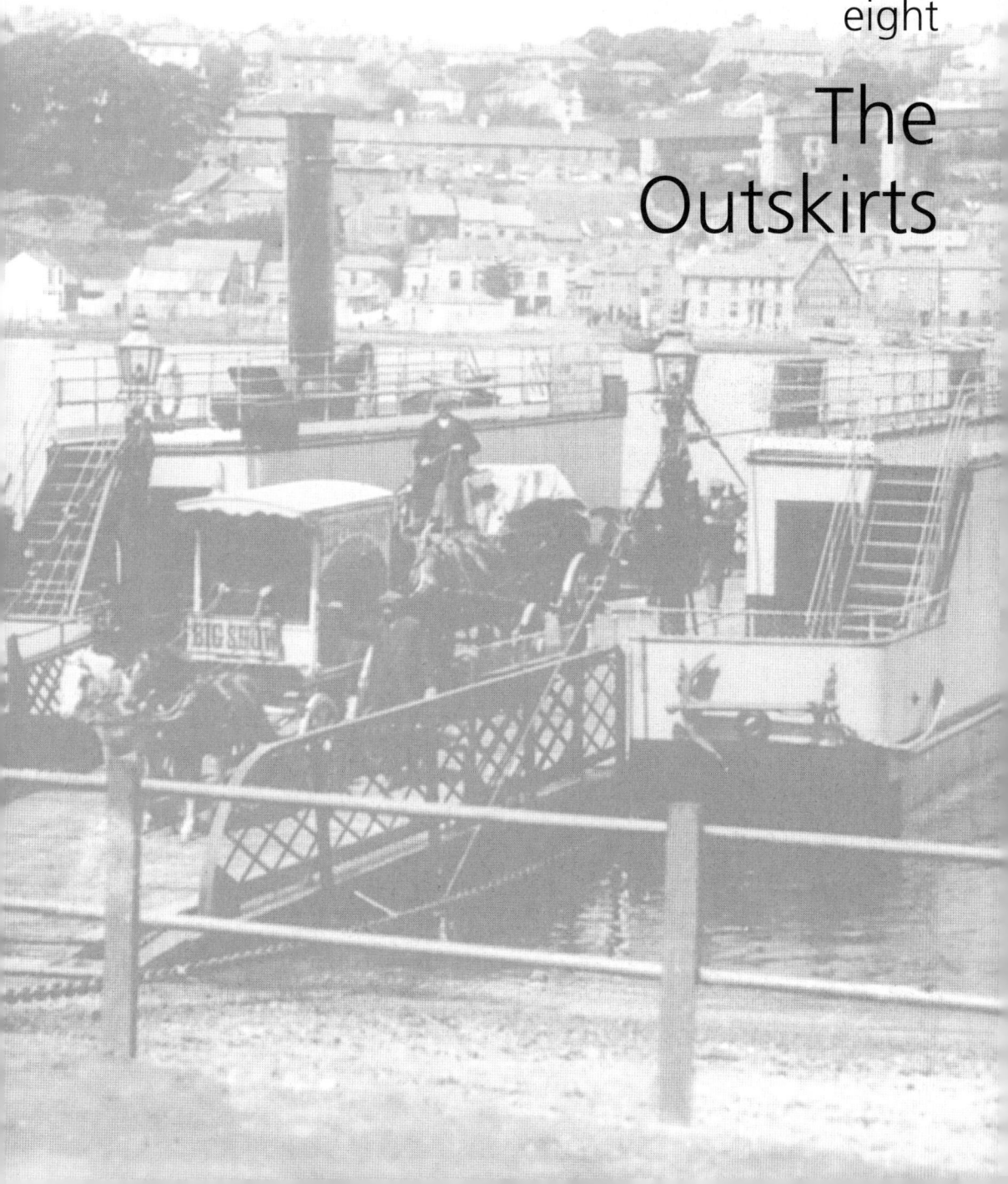

Trelawny Hotel and terrace, St Budeaux Square, *c.* 1910. The area is still recognisable today though the advent of cars and an increasing population has made this a very busy area. The building directly to the right of the hotel was once a coaching stable. General John Jago Trelawney who owned the Barne Estate sold this site to Joseph Stribling for £167 and the hotel was built in 1895. The Trelawney Hotel is still there and is still a public house.

Higher Lea Terrace, St Budeaux, *c.* 1910. Located at the top of Higher St Budeaux, this road and its houses have changed little in the last hundred years. The shop seen on the right was owned by W. Tozer and was St Budeaux's post office.

Above: Tamar Terrace, St Budeaux, *c.* 1920. Still very recognisable today, all of these buildings still remain though more houses have been built on the left of the picture. For years, this road was the main route for car travellers to the Tamar Bridge but with the building of the Parkway, the road was shut off at the far end.

Right: Maurice Dart watering plants in his garden at 16 Tamar Terrace, St Budeaux, in the 1930s. Tamar Terrace was renamed Normandy Way after the Second World War servicemen who marched this way to leave for the Normandy D-Day landings from Saltash Passage.

St Budeaux Foundation School, 1939. Headmaster Ewart Prior is seen here with Miss Packer, the class teacher. Maurice Dart is in the back row, second from the left. The school was founded in 1717. It was originally located at the village green at Higher St Budeaux but was rebuilt in 1876 at the top of Victoria Road. It was demolished in the early 1980s when the new road to the Tamar Bridge was built.

St Budeaux School infants, 1937. The headmaster is Mr Ewart Prior and the teacher Miss Ingram. Maurice Dart is in the third row, third from left. Mr Prior was a very popular headmaster and his brother was headmaster of a nearby school.

Ernesettle Road, *c.* 1910. These houses still stand and they would not be too difficult to recognise today for a visitor from the early twentieth century. However, traffic has increased significantly and in the distance, where open countryside and the River Tamar are visible, the Parkway now cuts through the land taking travellers to Cornwall over the Tamar Bridge.

Building of the Royal Albert Bridge, 1857. Designed by Isambard Kingdom Brunel, the bridge is 2,200ft long and has two main spans of 455ft, each weighing 1,060 tons. The total construction cost was £255,000. Brunel died shortly after its construction in September 1859, aged fifty-three.

The Saltash Ferry, c. 1905. The ferry was originally known as the Ashe–Torre Passage. Ashtorre was the old name for Saltash and the Saltash Passage side was known as Esses Torre. The road that runs behind the Royal Albert Bridge Inn has been the main route to Cornwall for centuries.

Right: The Royal Albert Bridge was opened on 2 May 1859 by HRH Prince Albert. Brunel was unable to attend due to illness but later saw the bridge shortly before his death.

Below: The Saltash Ferry, *c.* 1900. Until the early twentieth century, Saltash Passage was part of Cornwall. There had been a ferry link from Saltash Passage, on the Plymouth side, to Saltash for 600 years and the Brunel Bridge marks the old route of the ferry. When Brunel completed the bridge in 1859, the ferry moved further down river, just in front of the Ferry Inn.

BRISTOL & EXETER RAILWAY.

VISIT

OF HIS ROYAL HIGHNESS

THE PRINCE CONSORT,

TO THE

OPENING

OF THE

ROYAL ALBERT BRIDGE,

AT

SALTASH,

ON

MONDAY, 2nd May, 1859.

ROYAL TRAIN TIME BILL.

DOWN.	DEP. A.M.	ARR. A.M.	UP.	DEP. P.M.	ARR. P.M.
WINDSOR	6 0		SALTASH	—	
Bristol		8 35	Cornwall Junction		—
"	8 45		"	6 50	
Taunton...		9 35	Newton		—
"	9 38		"	—	
Exeter		10 25	Exeter		8 15
"	10 35		"	8 25	
Newton		11 5	Taunton...		9 12
"	11 10		"	9 15	
Cornwall Junction		12 0	Bristol		10 5
"	12 5		"	10 15	
SALTASH		12 15	WINDSOR		12 50

The following arrangements will be necessary for the proper working of this Train, which must be strictly attended to:—

The 7.50 a.m. Down Passenger Train is to Shunt at Tiverton Junction.
The 8.0 a.m. Goods Train Down will not start from Bristol until after the Royal Train.
The 8.0 p.m. Up Train is to Shunt at Tiverton Junction.
The 9.20 p.m. Short Train from Weston is to Shunt at Yatton.

Barron, 29th April, 1859.

SALTASH BRIDGE.

Opposite above: The Saltash Ferry at Saltash Passage, 1920s. The main way to get over to Saltash and Cornwall if travelling by car was either by the ferry or driving all the way around via Gunnislake. As more and more people got cars, this route to Cornwall got busier and busier until the Tamar Bridge was finally built in 1961.

Left: Mauice Dart at Saltash Passage steps, 1930s. These steps are still there and lead down to the shore beside the children's park underneath the bridge. Here, a young Maurice Dart decides whether or not to go in for a paddle.

Below: A tram at Saltash Passage, *c.* 1923. Saltash Passage would have been the last stop by the river before this tram headed off back into the town. In 1923, the line was extended from St Budeaux along a track that had been closed since the First World War. The trip from the pier to Saltash Passage covered a remarkable nine miles and was the longest journey in the city. The fare was 4d. This one is marked 'Theatre' and its final destination would have been by Derry's Clock.

A truck belonging to Webber Ltd boards the Saltash Ferry by the Royal Albert Bridge in the 1920s. The Royal Albert Bridge Inn is on the right. The tea gardens at Saltash Passage, known as Little Ash Gardens, were described as 'Devonport's Beauty Spot' and featured swings, a roundabout and see-saws. Combined with the St Budeaux Regatta on the Tamar, the tea gardens boasted 20,000 visitors in one summer. The Tramways Band would play there and the tea gardens were promoted as offering 'High Class Teas and Refreshments at Popular Prices'.

Acknowledgements

Thanks to Maurice Dart and his extensive collection of photographs, Eric Webb, Madeleine Slater, W.H. Burgoyne, Tina Cole, John and Joyce Cole, Florence Colton, Ivy Graddon, Marshall and Sally Ware, the Park Pharmacy Trust, Derek Gigg, Eileen Cock, Neil Hinkley, Bob and Helen Williams, Brian Moseley and A.J. Marriot for all their help and for supplying photographs for this publication.

Thanks also to H.J. Heinz Company Ltd, Mumford's, the New Continental Hotel, Jaeger, Goodbody's, the Duke of Cornwall Hotel, the Grand Hotel and Boots for their permission to use the advertisements featured in this publication.

I have done my best to track down the owners of the copyright for all images used and apologise to anyone not mentioned.

I would be interested to hear from anyone who has old photographs, advertisements, documents etc. concerning Plymouth that could be used in future publications. I am particualy interested in items from the early 1900s until the late 1970s. Please contact me at: Derek Tait, PO Box 7, West Park, Plymouth, PL5 2YS or email me at: derek.tait@virgin.net

Bibliography

Publications
Fleming, Guy, *Plymouth: A Pictorial History* (Phillimore & Co. Ltd, 1995)
— , *A Century of Plymouth* (Sutton Publishing, 2000)
Langley, Martin and Small, Edwina, *The Trams of Plymouth* (Libris Press, 1992)
— , *Millbay Docks* (Devon Books, 1987)
Marriot, A.J., *Laurel and Hardy – The British Tours* (A.J. Marriott, 1993)
Moseley, Brian, 'Through the Lens' series (Brian Moseley, 1989-1993)
Robinson, Chris, *As Time Draws On* (Pen and Ink Publishing, 1985)
— , *Union Street* (Pen and Ink Publishing, 2000)
Ware, Marshall, *The Ancient Parish of St Budeaux* (Arthur Clamp, 1983)

Newspapers
Evening Herald
Western Morning News

Websites
Brian Moseley's Plymouth Data website at www.plymouthdata.info
Steve Johnson's Cyberheritage website at www.cyberheritage.co.uk
Wheal Martyn website at www.wheal-martyn.com
Applause Southwest at www.applausesw.org.uk